THE MAAFA & BEYOND

BY

ERRIEL D. ROBERSON

The Maafa & Beyond
Remembrance, Ancestral Connections and Nation Building
for the African global community

by Erriel D. Roberson

KUJICHAGULIA PRESS ■ Columbia, MD

ISBN : 0-9644932-0-9

Library of Congress Catalog Card Number: 94-74578

Cover Art Copyright © 1995 by Stanley E. Brown

Cover Design by Larry Bradshaw of ONA Design

For more information contact:

KUJICHAGULIA   PRESS
9506 Ridgeview Dr.
Columbia, MD 21046
(410) 880-4354

Dedicated to the memory of Papa A. C.

Acknowledgements

Praise is due to the Creator for having blessed me with good friends, a large and loving extended family, and the most wonderful wife in the world. Special thanks to Larry, Ruth and Jay, all of whom came through in the crunch. Also, Marlise Brown, here's to you.

CONTENTS

PREFACE

This book has been a natural progression for me as an author and as an individual participant in the struggle for the physical and mental liberation of African people. The nature of writing for liberation dictates that I have matured in terms of the knowledge of myself, my history, my culture and my direction in our struggle.

The Maafa & Beyond has a vital place in the future of African people. As we find ourselves still bound by mental and physical fetters, this book will contribute to our continued rise to a position of peace, self-determination, balance, truth, self-definition and greatness.

In terms of our mental fetters, it is fairly clear and recognized that we as African people have been manipulated in the way of miseducation, propaganda and cultural devaluation. The majority of us attend schools run by people and institutions that have never had our best interests in mind and have been quite hostile toward us. There is also never a shortage of negative images and psychological battery that we have to endure.

Physically, we remain dependent on others for our sustenance, whether it be economic viability, land ownership, protection, food production or any number of areas in which a people who want to be free must be self-sustaining.

The Maafa & Beyond is an important addition to the body of work that serves to take us, as an African people, to the place of prominence in the world we are capable of. This book offers suggested solutions. Defining problems without producing viable solutions is useless. We should attempt to live according to the knowledge we gather and the precepts that we read and write about.

I have written, prior to this book, about the need for African people to define themselves and not be defined by others. The title of this book serves to redefine and reclaim our history. The Swahili term "Maafa" is explained in the introduction and I am indebted to Marimba Ani for her use of that term in her book, *Yurugu*. Essential in my use of the term is that it signifies an African term being used by African people to define our history of enslavement and suffering. This is my way of contributing to our definition of ourselves as African people. The logic behind this use of language as a liberating force is dealt with in the text of this work.

When we talk about our enslavement, the initial reaction for many African people is to shy away from the subject, believing we have already talked about "slavery" too much or we have run the issue into the ground. However, I dare say that most who take this stance know little more about the experience than the requisite line concerning our loss of culture, language, families, religion, etc. This is by no means an adequate nor complete knowledge of our suffering. Therefore, much of our initial reaction to conversations about our enslavement is an indoctrinated mind-set which devalues our suffering, makes us believe that it is over and anything more to be said about it is simply complaining. Because our history texts deal with even less than the requisite information mentioned above, we think we know all there is to know and buy into the view that we are complaining if we continue to speak on our suffering.

I challenge these views. I would say that most of us should be embarrassed by the paucity and superficiality of the knowledge we do have about this great disaster of ours. I also maintain that those of us who have a bit more in-depth and critical knowledge than others are often still viewing this suffering from someone else's perspective, using someone else's terms and definitions. This book addresses this problem and many more aspects of our existence as African people.

The subtitle; *Remembrance, Ancestral Connections and Nation Building for the African Global Community*, is easily defined in terms of its significance and meaning. "Remembrance" means to remember, but more importantly it means a celebration or honor of the memory of our ancestors and the events that have shaped our collective existence. "Ancestral Connections" refers to the attempt in this work to illuminate the ways in which African people around the world share a common destiny based on our origins and relationships due to common suffering. "Nation Building for the African Global Community" means to think as one nation of people with a common agenda and act accordingly.

We all have different contributions to the struggle and levels at which we will contribute in it. I have much confidence in the future. There are developments in our African community from positive brothers and sisters that are exciting and productive. We are on the verge of a huge movement towards greatness. I hope that I have contributed something to this movement.

Peace and Blessings,
Erriel D. Roberson
January 16, 1995

▲
INTRODUCTION

The greatest memorial that can be to the people of the
middle passage (while I call for and strongly suggest a physical
memorial in addition to a museum of slavery, preserving the orna-
mentations, the chains, and atrocities so that our children will know
that it wasn't easy) would be to remind them of the work they still have
to do.

Your mission is to remember and to teach your children so that
they can remember it.
> John Henrik Clarke, <u>Christopher Columbus &</u>
> <u>the Afrikan Holocaust</u>

The question still remains, will we define our struggle for
ourselves or continuously be defined by our enemy? Our major
problem is ourselves--is our inability to come to a workable conclusion
as to what we are struggling for and whom we are struggling against
or even with, for that matter. Our thinking on this issue is fuzzy,
unclear like the polluted water we drink. And, just as the water slowly
kills us physically, our inactivity as a people kills us mentally and
spiritually. But, we must struggle--even if our means and our
analysis of the struggle are in conflict--it is best, in these times, to
struggle with conflict than not to struggle at all. Out of conflict comes
clarity or destruction--we have a choice.
> Haki Madhubuti, <u>Enemies: the clash of the</u>
> <u>races</u>

This work is a memorial. This work is for remembrance and
understanding. This work is for creating doers and nation builders in the

3

vast potential of the oppressed African masses.

This book could be viewed as two separate concepts, intricately bound by the common thread of struggle. First, the tragedy of human suffering that has been referred to as the African Slave Trade will be dealt with, placing this ordeal within an African-centered framework. This book is not being written to analyze this tragedy as commerce or international trade, as so many have done who have written on the subject. This is for us; those who suffered and those who were lost. We must mourn and deal with the pain in order to move on. We must hold this tragedy before the world. A traumatic event in life or in one's family must be mourned and remembered. That is healthy and natural. On the other hand, to forget or block out the memory, with no tears or sadness, is psychologically harmful, unnatural and unhealthy.

At this point in time, the masses of African[1] people throughout the diaspora have not dealt with this great tragedy. Many of our African brothers and sisters, as well as other people, have no idea of the immensity of this great disaster. Most don't know of the lasting effects, including the colonization of Africa, that followed our enslavement and continues to shape the chaos on that continent; not to mention the psychological impact on African people world wide and on those other peoples who participated in the event. There are others who are ashamed of this historical legacy, often because of the negative and false images of pickaninnies and sambos, as well as the romanticized historical images of passive Africans content with their condition. They are not familiar with the widespread revolutionary resistance throughout the diaspora and on the continent.

Our lack of knowledge concerning our enslavement also affects our ability to see the foundations for our worldwide unity. Far too many African people in America see themselves as somehow different from Africans elsewhere, even from those on the continent! This is part of the pathology of historical ignorance, which can be well on the way to being remedied when we truly understand how we got here, what has shaped our existence, and from where we have come. However, there can be no remedy if we do not have the "medicine" of understanding our condition.

We have no national museum and we have not defined the tragedy from our own perspective. School textbooks inadequately address the issue when addressing it at all and we do not hold anyone accountable in order to ensure that this horrible past ceases to influence our present global condition. There are a few who have begun this work and hopefully this piece will further the cause.

The second aspect of this book deals with our mobilization as a people, our unity and our activities on the road to self-determination and self-sufficiency. It is in this part of the book that we deal with some of the pressing issues of our day and propose measures for confronting every-thing that stands in our way as we rise. This is where we come to grips with our existence of oppression throughout the world and formulate plans of action because we are not victims, though we have been victimized. This is where we fashion ourselves as an African world community capable of upturning the foundations of a world hostile to our being.

This book is a combination of scholarship, inspiration, critical historical understanding and memory. However, there are also some basic issues that are of extreme importance, regarding our use of language, which must be dealt with at the outset.

❖ The importance of language ❖

There are many who don't recognize the importance of language, or the spoken word. What we say is the articulation of thought. What we say, or the language we use, is the bringing of thought into the realm of reality.

This importance, which is attached to the spoken word, has re-sounded throughout history. In the spiritual philosophy of the ancient African people of Kemet (Egypt), "the tongue is the organ which creates the conceived thought as a phenomenal actuality." [2]

In the ancient scriptures of Kemet, in one book of scriptures de-scribing creation it reads "Many were the beings that came forth from the commands of my mouth." [3] In the Holy Bible of the Christian faith, the book of 1 John states that, "In the beginning there was the Word and the Word was God." Then, if one is to look in Genesis "God said, 'Let there be light'; and there was light." God goes on to command creation with the spoken word.

The importance of "the word" is no less crucial in every aspect of life. We are dealing with what has been called the "African Slave Trade" here. The precise use of words is powerful and critical. The very term, "African Slave Trade," is inadequate for the remembrance and memorialization of our great tragedy. Slavery is a generic term that de-scribes a condition of bondage that has existed in various forms through-out recorded history. As a generic term, it is not an adequate descriptor for our great tragedy, which was different and more devastating than any form of slavery in the history of the world. Trade is an equally generic term which implies business or bartering and the selling of commodities. It is blasphemous to regard human suffering and death as selling com-modities or doing business. Perhaps this was the degrading attitude of slavers, and even some of those who write on the subject today, but we must REFUSE to cast it in such a callous and disrespectful light. This use of words insures that the impact of the so called "African Slave Trade" will be viewed more in terms of commerce and just another event in the age old tradition of bondage, rather than the horrific and uniquely significant event that it was. It would be akin to calling the Jewish Holocaust something as crass and inappropriate as "The Great European Cleansing Project."

This book will, from this point, cease to refer to the "African Slave Trade" except where it is necessary for citing sources or clarifying quoted text. Instead, the term coined by Marimba Ani in her book *Yurugu* will be used. Ani, who thoroughly understands the use of language, used the Swahili term, "Maafa." Maafa is defined as a disaster, calamity, damage, injustice, misfortune, catastrophe, etc. Ani referred to it as "the Maafa, the great suffering of our people at the hands of Europeans in the Western Hemisphere." [4] This use of the term does not shy away from the predominant role of Europeans in the Maafa, just as the Jewish Holocaust does not shy away from the predominant role of Germans. This is just factual reality. Our only modification to the use of the term is that we will not confine it to the Western hemisphere, due to the tremendous loss of life before the arrival of our ancestors in this hemisphere. Secondly, we will use the term, "Great Suffering" (always capitalized), interchangeably with Maafa. The use of Great Suffering to define this historical tragedy is as valid as the use of Great Depression to describe the economic tragedy in American history.

From this point on we will be using the terms Maafa and Great Suffering. Unlike the use of "African Slave Trade," both Maafa and Great Suffering implicitly connote the pain, horror and injustice of our experience. This is as it should be and it is hoped that in *every* instance where people have occasion to speak of this experience of African people, they will refer to it as the Maafa or Great Suffering. Initially this will mean that those who use the terms will have to be adept at articulating what they mean and why the terms should be used, but this is worth it. It is worth it for us and our ancestors.

Given our analysis of language, the inappropriate nature of currently used words such as "import," "export," "commercial trade," etc., has no place in our reverence for and remembrance of the Maafa. To give an example of the changing of perspective regarding language use in this book, "kidnapping" is one term that will be used in place of such terms as import, export, migration, etc.

With regard to language and words, I hope that the power of the spoken and written word is not lost on this book and the Great Suffering alone. This is the kind of revolutionary shift in consciousness that must be applied to all aspects of life in order for any group of oppressed people to be free. It is the liberating act of ceasing to allow those that oppress to define the oppressed. It is self-definition and self-determination, without which one remains dependent and weak. Haki Madhubuti in his latest work, *Claiming Earth*, elucidates this issue of language when he shares his views.

> That is why oppressed people communicating in English
> must conquer it and proceed with deliberate speed and accuracy to
> carve out their own territory of self-expression and visions of a bright
> tomorrow. Language is a code. Learn to use it, or be used by it. [5]

❖ *General overview* ❖

As mentioned, part of the function of this book is to serve as a memorial to the Great Suffering. Therefore, the areas of concentration in this book are not designed to focus on the actions and motives of those outside the group of sufferers, whether these were anti-Maafa fighters or perpetrators of the event. This is not to exclude or deny their significance, but this book is for us; those who suffered and those who were lost.

The first part of the work is entitled "The Maafa" and deals with several areas. First we come to grips with the immensity of the Maafa, in terms of the sheer numbers of lives involved. Currently in the world of academia, there is much activity and debate over how many millions of African people were part of the Maafa; specifically, how many were kidnapped from the continent and how many arrived alive in the Western hemisphere. This flurry of activity will be examined and put into perspective. This will aid in grasping the enormous dimensions of the Great Suffering and the memorialization of our ancestors.

From the examination of the numbers of Africans kidnapped and murdered, we will move on to get first hand accounts of the suffering our ancestors endured. From this point we will explore the dispersion of Africans and where they were taken throughout the world. The importance of understanding the origin of African people around the globe will aid in making vital connections with those people for the purpose of cooperative struggle, as well as global thinking and identification with African people worldwide. Because this section of the book is taking a look at Africans worldwide, it will be necessary to look at areas of the world, outside of Africa, where direct African connections remain from the time of the kidnapping during the Maafa. Examples are the Gullahs of the Sea Islands, off the coast of South Carolina and Georgia, who have retained much of the culture and some language of their African forebears; and the African communities of Brazil who maintain African language, as well as cultural traditions. Many more such connections are presented and their significance explained.

The spirit of resistance is the subject matter for the fourth chapter of part one. African resistance to and triumph over the Maafa will be viewed, with emphasis on numerous insurrections, revolutions, Maroon societies and heroes of these struggles. Special emphasis will be given to the triumphant struggles, such as those in Suriname, Jamaica, Haiti, and Florida (Africans in the Seminole nation), under the leadership of such heroes as Toussaint L'Overture, Dessalines, Cudjoe, Joseph Cinque and Acheampong Nanny. The sophisticated and "near miss" plans of people such as Denmark Vesey, Gabriel Prosser and Nat Turner will also be memorialized. The additional component will be the later resistance of great orators and spokespeople such as Frederick Douglass, David Walker, Ida B. Wells, Henry Highland Garnet, etc.

In part two the aftermath of the Maafa will be discussed with an eye on its lasting effects, including the resultant European colonization of Africa in the late 1800's, lynching, psychological depravation, and economic devastation in America and around the world. This second part of the book is entitled "The Aftermath: Beyond the Maafa." Positives like Pan-Africanism, Nationalist movements, and personalities such as the Honorable Marcus Mosiah Garvey and the Honorable Elijah Muhammad will be remembered. Of extreme importance is the chapter that deals with nation building and offers direction for action, as well as a vision for the future.

The third part of the book is entitled "Critical After-Thinking." Practical and specific issues such as teaching the Maafa, further investigations into language, a look at population politics and an examination of cultural reclamation in music constitute critical essays that finish this section. These essays function as ammunition for the continuing attacks on the humanity of African people and the righteousness of our struggle.

The final section of this work is entitled "Healing Time." Insights on psychological scars from the Maafa, their remedies and models for continued nation building finish the text.

The extensive material covered in this book is relevant to our continued struggle. It is intended to be a coherent and logical progression of ideas and information. The student, as well as the teacher should be able to draw something of substance from these pages. There are fresh ideas in addition to pieces of well known data, and there is an intangible spirit which weaves its thread throughout the book's content and purpose. It is the spirit of remembrance, reverence, respect, resistance, love, pride, divine light, self-determination, righteous intention and persistent struggle.

❖ *Perspectives and direction* ❖

This work on the Maafa, the Great Suffering, should serve as a shifter of paradigms and another of the catalysts for the reclamation of African history and African minds. It will be an example of how true liberation of thought and speech is empowering, enlightening and inspirational. The importance of reclaiming our history is enormous and the reclamation of the Maafa, since most of live in exile from the African continent because of it, is a monumental step in the continuing surge of self determination, mental health and mental wealth in the African community. Dr. Na'im Akbar, from his own professional and cultural perspective as an African psychologist, informs us that:

> Slavery was 'legally' ended in excess of 100 years ago, but the
> 300 years experienced in its brutality and unnaturalness constituted a
> severe psychological and social shock to the minds of African
> Americans. This shock was so destructive to natural life processes that
> the current generation of African-Americans, though we are 5-6
> generations removed from the actual experience of slavery, still carry
> the scars of this experience in both our social and mental lives.
> Psychologists and sociologists have failed to attend to the persistence
> of problems in our mental and social lives which clearly have their
> roots in slavery.[6]

So it is clear that this book has a significance that goes far beyond that of recounting history, but reaches into our psychological processes. It is offered as a healing elixir or salve for African people.

The continuum of historical processes stemming from the Maafa also, when clearly understood, serve as our launching pad for global struggle and real liberation. For a very long time African people have been able to articulate the problems that we face as a people. Often times the few who have moved on this analysis have made mistakes in strategies or miscalculations of objectives and the definition of freedom. It is from these experiences that we are able to learn and take the struggle a step further. Our objectives are clear and we have matured to the realization that there can be no freedom if a people does not control their psychological processes through education and media, their economic sustenance, their culture, and the definitions and views they assign to the world. We will make mistakes, but not the same mistakes that have been made before.

History has been a harsh teacher for African people. Harsh teachers give harsh lessons, and ours is that there is no middle road or peaceful coexistence devoid of constant, intense struggle. We cannot and do not wish to assimilate into American or Western culture. We must, and will, deal with it from a comfortable position of equity and African cultural grounding. Not only does assimilation mean that we would attempt to adopt the values of the most corrupt, manipulating, and violent cultural group on the earth (history as a witness), but that cultural group we call Europeans doesn't want extra baggage. This is a good thing, because too many of us are begging to be extra baggage rather than equitable counterparts. European resistance aids those of us who believe we should bring something of our own to the table of the world instead of remaining on the floor asking for crumbs from the plates of others.

Every time we allow ourselves to be lulled into a comfortable slumber with the state of the world for African people, we are guaranteed a slap in the face from the societies and institutions that won't let us forget that we are not welcome. Racist theories show their faces in cycles and seem to capture the warm sentiments of the masses of Europeans every time. At the very least, one would expect some type of mass outrage by our European counterparts at the constant attacks on Africans, if we were meant to "fit" into a European dominated world. However, the same conspicuous lack of sufficient outrage or support, that allowed the Maafa to be our experience for hundreds of years, is the case every time we fall under the attack of negative media barrages, physical assaults, documented incidences of discrimination, or pseudo-academic/pseudo-scientific racism. We never get the ground swell of intolerance and support that we would get from a society that accepts us as equals and welcomes us.

It is not our place to be as patient and forgiving as we have been. No other group of people on the face of the earth has exhibited the patience that we have and attempts to live harmoniously with oppressors, most foolishly. We are being tempered in the fire though. We are being tempered for greatness again.

Our road ahead will not be an easy one. It is no stretch of the imagination to say that African people around the world are engaged in a war. In the many wars that make up the history of humanity, people have always allied with others having common interests. Great nations have put aside ideological disagreements that become minuscule trifles in the face of impending destruction. In like manner, African people around the

10

world must become allies with one another. Making this all the more difficult is the fact that from many corners deliberate mechanisms are in place to undermine African global unity. Given this fact, African people who are conscious must employ mechanisms that counterattack outsiders and arm their brothers and sisters at the same time. This is where we are with this book.

Unfortunately, there is not time, in books such as this one, to lay out the ways in which we are at war. We now approach the crossroads and that dictates that we pay attention to what it is we will do for ourselves. The record of those who operate against us is acknowledged, documented and will continue to be documented. That allows for others of us to be about the business of preparing responses, remedies and proactive action for liberation.

This is not to say that we will not need volumes of work yet to come that will keep us abreast of the problems we face and who should be held accountable. What is being said is that we must be balanced in our approach. We can no longer afford to cry "foul" while sitting still. The Civil Rights movement has shown us definitively that our oppressors do not flinch at accusations of their lack of moral character, their cruelty, etc. Dr. Martin Luther King's appeal to the moral consciousness of America has done little to change attitudes and actions of America's oppressive apparatuses. As we sang "We Shall Overcome," the dogs continued to bite, the water continued to flow from the hoses, institutions maintained their racist infrastructure and police batons continued to crack African skulls. All respect is due to the accomplishments of this movement. All respect is due to those of our people who suffered, bled and died during this movement so that my generation and those to follow might live better lives. With all that was accomplished, the fact remains that none of what was achieved came about by simply pointing out the faults of an oppressive society to that society. What success the movement achieved came as a result of mobilization, political pressure, the oppressed masses hearing the accusations hurled at the oppressors, and the masses becoming aware of their oppression as a result. The opening of our eyes by the likes of Malcolm X is an example of this last point.

In short, there is little to be found in this book in the way of pointing out who has done what to us. Instead, the other side of the issue is addressed, which is looking at what has happened to us and how we will move on that reality. The lack of attention paid to our oppressors peculiar attitudes and tendencies is not by any means to be mistaken for letting them off the hook. There is in fact some dealing with European psychological processes; however, this book takes for granted that we realize that many external factors contributed, and continue to contribute, to our condition, but what is that condition and what do we do now? Move on African people, move on.

In order to fully grasp the magnitude of our current problems, we must reopen the books on the events of slavery. Our objective should not be to cry stale tears for the past, nor to rekindle old hatreds for past injustices. Instead, we should seek to enlighten our path of today by better understanding where and how the lights were turned out yesterday.

Na'im Akbar, Chains and Images of Psycho-logical Slavery

PART I
THE MAAFA (GREAT SUFFERING)

▲
Chapter 1

The Suffering of Millions

Stripped entirely naked, the slaves were packed into the stinking holds of the ships so close together that they were forced to sleep on their sides. With manacles on both their hands and feet, the slaves were then linked together by a continuous chain bolted to the floor. Most would spend the entirety of what was often a two to three month journey in this position. A few, depending on the mind or mood of the captain, would see the deck and daylight during meal time or during other specified periods such as the tortuously cruel exercise period when the slaves were made to dance in their heavy, cutting shackles.

> Joseph Harris, ed., <u>Global Dimensions of the African Diaspora</u>

It is truly difficult to imagine the millions of Africans victimized in the Maafa. Even today, it is impossible to know exactly how many millions of human beings were "loose packed" or "tight packed" into the holds of ships. Information is even more fleeting on the millions who died before reaching the coast or while in holding pens waiting to be transferred to the ships to meet their horrible fate. Dr. John Henrik Clarke has said that one must begin counting at 60 million![1]

This is enough to send chills down the spines of the most non-feeling individuals. To think that number of human beings could be impacted by one traumatic and heinous historical process is almost inconceivable.

Currently, there is great debate taking place over the numbers of Africans who were victimized in the Great Suffering, for reasons that will be examined later on in this work. This debate is largely in the academic realm, generally far from the public domain, amongst scholars who endeavor to calculate estimates of the total number of Africans "exported," or kidnapped as we shall describe the ordeal. A key word here is *estimate*. No one knows how many lives were destroyed by their being transplanted or murdered during the Great Suffering. This is evident in the testimony of virtually every person who proposes to be a scholar on the subject. It is therefore important to take a meticulous look at what is taking place in the area of estimating the many millions of lives caught up in the Great Suffering.

Of the names of researchers that appear regularly on the topic of the Maafa, Joseph Inikori says "Given the nature of the evidence, it is clear that the true figure of people exported from Africa by way of the Atlantic trade cannot be produced by anyone." [2] David Henige says,

> ... no global estimate of the slave trade, or of any 'under-development' or 'underpopulation' it may have caused, are possible, though carefully constructed micro-studies might provide limited answers. Under the circumstances, to believe or advocate any particular set or range of figures becomes an act of faith rather than an epistemologically sound decision. [3]

Philip Curtin is significant with regard to estimates on the Maafa since most people in the circle of the current academic debate, including Inikori, use Curtin's estimates as a point of departure in one way or another. Consequently, Philip Curtin's thoughts are telling when he writes:

> One danger in stating numbers is to find them quoted later on with a degree of certitude that was never intended... They are not intended to be precise as given, only approximations where a result falling within twenty per cent of actuality is a "right" answer--that is, a successful result, given the quality of the underlying data. It should also be understood that some estimates will not even reach that standard of accuracy. [4]

Thus, having clearly established the uncertainty of the estimates, one might wonder exactly what data allows scholars to formulate their estimates and how many millions of people have they estimated to have been victims of the Great Suffering?

First, the type of data that is used to estimate the numbers of Africans kidnapped. Joseph Inikori says there are five types of evidence used in scholarly methodology.

(1) private or official accounts of export and import trade: commodities exported, slaves exported or imported, the number or tonnage of ships cleared out, slaves carried per ship or per ton, slave prices on the African coast, etc.;

(2) quantitative observations made by the slave traders on the African coast;

(3) systematic estimates made by contemporary writers on the basis of then existing primary data;

(4) well-informed guestimates by the slave traders;

(5) educated guestimates by contemporary writers who were much acquainted with the slave trade. [5]

Philip Curtin further enlightens us by describing his use of primary evidence.

The most obvious and direct kind of evidence is a systematic record of slaves imported through a particular port or into a given colony over a period of years. Such evidence exists, but only for a small fraction of the total slave trade. Equivalent direct evidence of imports is still more rare. [6]

James Rawley also gives an interesting synopsis. He writes of the time period between 1761 and 1808.

The sources for estimating the volume of the North American slave-carrying trade in this half-century are diverse and spotty. They include newspapers, naval officer's lists, contemporary estimates and statements, a list of exports from the Gold Coast for 1761-1768, and United States customs entries for 1804-07. Beyond this, inferences may be made... [7]

Given all of the above information, it is clear that untold millions suffered and the only value estimates can provide is to give general minimums of millions while no maximum amount can be established, beyond numerical impossibilities. This is especially true when the mortality rates are considered for Africans before embarking ships; an issue which will be discussed later. These mortality rates are usually not taken into account by estimates. Therefore, although the people doing calculations, who consider themselves scholarly authorities on the subject, may ridicule estimates like John Henrik Clarke's 60 million, they have no foundation to do so.

This brings us to a point where it is possible to look at the estimates of these scholars and understand the context from which they arise. These estimates are "export" estimates, meaning the numbers of Africans kidnapped who actually embarked ships leaving Africa. Again, the point that deserves stress is that these are "export" estimates.

Paul Lovejoy places his estimate at 11,698,000. [8] Joseph Inikori suggests a number around 15.4 million. [9] James Rawley's figures are 11, 345,000. [10] Philip Curtin's "import" estimate in his 1969 work, that spurred much of today's calculated estimates, is 9, 566,100.[11]

An important note to make at this time is, that with the exception of Philip Curtin who gives "import" figures, the above scholars are giving "export" number estimates. These estimates only account for the number of Africans kidnapped from that continent and bound for the Western hemisphere. Such estimates don't allow for another important aspect of the Maafa. One must also account for the mortality rate of Africans on their trek to the coast and during their inhumane internment in coastal slave forts before embarking ships. The numbers of people involved would seemingly escalate significantly if these mortality rates would be figured into the calculations of those attempting to arrive at estimates, but these scholars are concerned with "export" and "import." They feel evidence, however little, supports their calculations.

However, noted historian, Lerone Bennett Jr. felt that "during this period Africa lost an estimated forty million people. Some twenty million of these men and women came to the New World." [12] Bennett's forty million, which represents a 50% mortality rate, is inclusive not only of those who died during the Middle Passage of the Great Suffering, but also those who died before embarking ships and enduring that horror. Another historian, Joseph C. Miller, is of the opinion that:

> Death rates rose at an increasing tempo as slaves flowed into the central channels of the slave trade, perhaps to catastrophic levels in the range of 400-600 per 1000 per annum by the time the slaves reached the coast. One experienced Luanda merchant reported that slavers toward the second half of the eighteenth century expected to lose about 40 percent of their captives to flight and death between the time they put them on ships in Luanda. [13]

Given this passage, it is apparent that Miller assumed between 40 and 60 percent of the Africans died before embarking ships and enduring the Middle Passage of the Great Suffering. Basil Davidson concluded that "So far as the Atlantic slave trade is concerned, it appears reasonable to suggest that in one way or another, before and after embarkation, it cost Africa at least fifty million souls." [14] Davidson goes on to suggest that this estimate is "certainly on the low side." [15] And, as we mentioned from the outset, the venerable Dr. John Henrik Clarke says we **BEGIN** at 60 million.

So, no matter what estimate one chooses, the one thing that remains the same is that millions upon millions of African people were victims of the brutalization, trauma and murder of the Maafa. It is within bounds to say that if only a single individual today were made to endure kidnapping, rape, separation from family and friends, the hold of a ship under horrific conditions, the brutality of whippings and mutilations, and all that was endured during the Maafa, the world would be outraged. Escalate the figure of one to millions and perhaps we then see the great necessity to pay homage to the memory of our African ancestors. When we speak of the memorialization of our ancestors in the Great Suffering, we are not talking about the representations of Africans in Colonial Williamsburg, Virginia for example. Colonial Williamsburg is a celebration of European colonial history with enslaved Africans as an unavoidable incidental, viewed from the perspective of those celebrating this European heritage. This is not memorialization.

When we speak of memorialization, we certainly aren't speaking of the insulting lack of quantity and quality of information on the Great Suffering that is found in the nation's schools. Our memorialization is the erecting of monuments, the building of museums, the celebration of days of remembrance, the development of appropriate curriculum materials covering the Great Suffering, the intensive study of the Great Suffering and our increased consciousness as a people. There can be no doubt that we must elevate the Maafa to its proper position of prominence in world history, so that the world's people can come to grips with it and be accountable. The Maafa must be a mirror to the world, so that the ugliness that persists even until today can be seen and not neatly stashed away. African people need to study the Maafa and be sure that we prevent its reoccurrence. By reoccurrence, we mean much more than the manifestation of physical enslavement again. Reoccurrence means all forms of exploitation, genocide, miseducation, rape, and brutal aggression of both the physical and intellectual type.

We owe it to our ancestors, ourselves and our unborn children. We will be waiting a very long time if we expect the world to hold a mirror to its ugliness on its own accord. Nations built on the murder and brutalization of millions, and the manipulation of information presented to its masses, have no reason to expose themselves and every reason to downplay the Maafa. Therefore, we must make people see what they do not wish to see, even those Africans in our midst who have been taught to be ashamed. We must resurrect this painful past if there is to be healing, learning and progress.

19

Instead of building more basketball courts for the government's proposed night basketball, we should be building museums and statues to honor our suffering. We should be talking about it and understanding that no one can tell you to just forget the memories of millions upon millions of people. Knowing the scope of this tragedy provides ammunition against those who would tell us to "forget about the past" or that "slavery is over." Not only Africans, but other people should be sorry and grief stricken whenever they think or hear of the Maafa. Formal apologies and compensation are also to be taken seriously. Both of which have been granted to other peoples of the world who have suffered. The United States still expects and accepts apologies from Japan on each anniversary of the bombing of Pearl Harbor. The Germans still lament and apologize to the European Jews for the Holocaust, at the demand of Jewish people. The United States payed reparations to Japanese Americans who were put in concentration camps during World War II. The list goes on, so apologies and reparations are not impossible or impractical where the Maafa is concerned.

Perhaps also, part of our healing is in knowing the immensity of the Maafa, as has been described in this chapter. Sometimes an adopted child will want to know who their real parents are; a mourning person might want to know how their loved one died; a student will want to know how many and which questions they failed to answer correctly on a test; a person who is sick will want to know what the diagnosis is and so on. These are unanswered questions that help individuals deal with their present situation if answered. Likewise, knowing of the millions who endured the Maafa might give us the relief of knowing. Also, it is logical that many who are suffering under the continued oppression of the African existence will probably get a feeling of legitimacy from knowing. That person can no longer be told that his or her condition is simply a function of personal, individual ineptitude which characterizes Africans disproportionately. With this knowledge, there is a realization that the Maafa, by sheer numbers, *had* to have shaped much of our current situation. Therefore it is realized that we're not supposed to be languishing as a people and as individuals. We should be getting up and doing something lest we willingly accept the enslavement that our ancestors fought against.

Finally, aside from all of the benefits of the knowledge of the numbers, there is something simply called Truth. The Truth must be told as a matter of principle. Regardless of religious affiliation or cultural beliefs, Truth is an integral and unavoidable concept. There is no viable belief system that doesn't at least claim that they believe in Truth. We as African people certainly must and will embrace a love for Truth.

Having dealt with the debate and scholarship concerning the

millions of people victimized in the Great Suffering, we must move forward. It is painful, but necessary, to listen to those who suffered describe the suffering they endured, in the next chapter.

Chapter 2

Our Ancestors Speak

The chattel slavery of Africans in America for over 300 years serves as one of the saddest commentaries on man's inhumanity to man. The tales of this period of our history are so morbid that they will arouse vehement hostilities at the very thought of what occurred.

Na'im Akbar, <u>Chains and Images of</u>
<u>Psychological Slavery</u>

What follows are narrative accounts of the experience of the Great Suffering through the voices of those who survived to share their story. This is the human side of suffering and pain. Often times an individual who has suffered a traumatic experience or painful loss will react by putting their hands to their ears to block out painful external noise or internal sounds of pain. The external noise might be sounds or voices that remind the person of the painful experience. The internal noise might be the mind replaying these external sounds or the mind beating itself up over what has taken place, through an internal voice we call our conscience.

In most instances individuals must come to terms with this particular type of pain or go crazy. In bringing these voices of our ancestors forward, let us not only read, but also hear these voices so that their sound becomes the pain before our own mental and spiritual healing.

Even this brief collection of narratives may be painful to read. If it is not, perhaps we are as numb to our suffering as our oppressors are to heeping it upon us. These are our ancestors. Let us place ourselves in their shoes as we deal with our collective pain.

They whipped my father 'cause he looked at a slave they killed and cried. [1]

Poor Hetty, my fellow slave, was very kind to me, and I used to call her my aunt; but she led a most miserable life, and her death was hastened (at least the slaves all believed and said so,) by the dreadful chastisement she received from my master during her pregnancy. It happened as follows. One of the cows had dragged the rope away from the stake to which Hetty had fastened it, and got loose. My master flew into a terrible passion, and ordered the poor creature to be stripped quite naked, notwithstanding her pregnancy, and to be tied up to a tree in the yard. He then flogged her as hard as he could lick, both with the whip and cow skin, till she was all over streaming with blood. He rested, and then beat her again and again. Her shrieks were terrible. The consequence was that poor Hetty was brought to bed before her time, and was delivered after severe labour of a dead child. [2]

The stench of the hold while we were on the coast was so intolerably loathsome, that it was dangerous to remain there for any time, and some of us had been permitted to stay on deck for the fresh air; but now that the whole ship's cargo were confined together, it became absolutely pestilential. The closeness of the place, and the heat of the climate, added to the number in the ship, which was so crowded that each had scarcely room to turn himself, almost suffocated us... The shrieks of the women and the groans of the dying, rendered the whole scene a horror almost inconceivable. [3]

I said to him "For God's sake! Have you bought my wife?" He said he had... He drew out a pistol and said that if I went near the wagon on which she was, he would shoot me... I have never seen her from that day to this. I loved her as I love my life. [4]

They built a long trough like a great long cradle and put all these babies in it every morning when the mothers come out to the field. It was set at the end of the rows under a big cottonwood tree. When they went at the other end of the row, all at once a cloud no bigger than a small spot came up and it grew fast, and it thundered and lightened as if the world were coming to an end, and the rain just came down in great sheets. And when it got so they could go to the other end of the field, that trough was filled with water and every baby in it was floating round in the water, drowned. [5]

24

Poor Daniel was lame in the hip, and could not keep up with the rest of the slaves; and our master would order him to be stripped and laid down on the ground, and have him beaten with a rod of rough briar till his skin was quite red and raw. He would then call for a bucket of salt, and fling upon the raw flesh till the man writhed on the ground like a worm, and screamed aloud with agony. This poor man's wounds were never healed, and I have often seen them full of maggots, which increased his torments to an intolerable degree. [6]

He threw her down on the ground, and after beating her severely, he took her up in his arms and flung her among the prickley-pear bushes, which are all covered over with sharp venomous prickles. By this her naked flesh was so grievously wounded, that her body swelled and festered all over, and she died a few days after. [7]

One cannot help but be moved by the suffering of our forebears. These beautiful African people, brutalized to a point difficult to imagine, are our foreparents. Sadness, anger, disbelief and agonizing reflection are all emotions quite natural and healthy for the children of the Great Suffering to have. Often times African people are quizzically asked why they are so angry, despite the fact that our masses are currently the most passive, patient and forgiving sufferers in the world. Let no one ever again question our anger in the face of the pain that has been described above, multiplied by millions.

The awesome suffering of millions is also evident in the descriptions of historians, and the writings of Maafa kidnappers and holders of enslaved Africans that follow.

When the women and girls are taken aboard a ship, naked, trembling, terrified, perhaps almost exhausted with cold, fatigue, and hunger, they are often exposed to wanton rudeness of white savages. [8]

I have seen them sentenced to unmerciful whippings, continued till the poor creatures have not had power to groan under the misery, and hardly a sign of life has remained. I have seen them agonizing for hours, I believe for days together, under the torture of the thumbscrews; a dreadful engine, which, if the screw be turned by an unrelenting hand, can give intolerable anguish. [9]

The most serious impediment to the man's acquisition of status in his family was his inability to protect his wife from the sexual advances of whites and the physical abuse of his master. [10]

The white man's pursuit of black women frequently destroyed any possibility that comely black girls could remain chaste for long. [11]

Generally speaking, the women were literally forced to offer themselves "willingly" and receive a trinket for their compliance rather than a flogging for their refusal or resistance. [12]

The strain was too much for tens and thousands, who died of old and new diseases and the shock of psychic mutilation. But millions of others, testifying to physical and spiritual strength that transcended the heroic, survived. [13]

For those of us who are the survivors and for all people, especially in this Western hemisphere, there is no escaping the memory of the Great Suffering. It is a tragic event that has touched every aspect of existence for all of us. Our understanding of just how many millions were kidnapped and an inkling as to the degree of the suffering is a beginning in stirring our memories. Having a memory that is whole and complete as an African person means having a complex and critical understanding of the Great Suffering, or Maafa. Just as a person with amnesia is doomed to walk around confused about who he or she is, where they have come from, where they are headed and the nature of their relationships with others, so to is the African who does not know, memorialize and understand the Great Suffering.

Our memory and understanding of the Maafa is a beginning to the piecing together of the larger picture of how African people came to be where they are in the world and why they have the relationships with others that they have. It is also coming to terms with a painful history. Thus, the implications can be viewed as two-fold from this perspective.

First, in order to reap the benefits of a full understanding of where we are today, we must have an uncompromised, unromanticized view of this seminal event in the shaping our existence. Secondly, in order to deal in a healthy and constructive manner with the pain of this history, we need to get all of it out. In other words, an uncompromised, unromanticized view of the Maafa is also necessary for our mental and spiritual well being.

This is compounded by the fact that only the Maafa in all of its horror and brutality can explain the root cause of many of the self-destructive and insane mind states that exist among African people, and even European people, worldwide. (Chapter 11 examines this further.)

Without an understanding of the enormous scope and unimaginably heinous continuum of the Maafa, it becomes easy for some to explain away certain behaviors and societal circumstances as the sole fault and problem of the children of the Maafa, African people.

Up to this point, we have addressed the enormity of the Great Suffering and its horrendous nature. Now let us move on to understand the connections between African people worldwide that are made clear by the Great Suffering.

Main Destinations of Kidnapped Africans During the Maafa

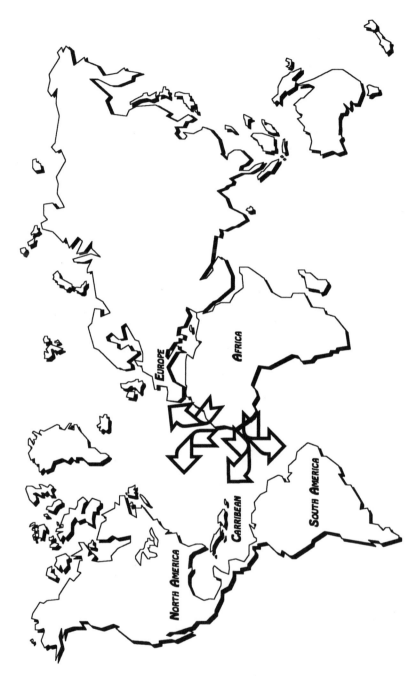

EUROPE

AFRICA

NORTH AMERICA

CARRIBEAN

SOUTH AMERICA

*By Far, the most Africans were taken to the Carribean and South America (Specifically Brazil).

Chapter 3

African Global Connections

The African diaspora assumes the character of a dynamic, continuous, and complex phenomenon stretching across time, geography, class and gender.

Joseph Harris, ed., <u>Global Dimensions of the</u> <u>African Diaspora</u>

African people around the world share a common oppression and a common ancestral culture and heritage. Whether they live in Brazil, the United States, Costa Rica, Panama, Cuba, Canada, Britain, Rwanda, Senegal, Kenya, Nigeria, Jamaica, Puerto Rico, the Bahamas, or any other place in the world, Africans all share Africa as their ancestral home and have all been affected by the Maafa. For those Africans in the United States, Brazil, Canada, the Caribbean and other locations in the Western hemisphere, who have not recently immigrated from Africa, the common link is that the Maafa has brought us all to be where we exist in the world. We share a history of suffering and pain.

The link between us in the Western hemisphere and those Africans on the continent is two fold; we all originated from the same place, which is Africa, and Africans on the continent have also suffered through the pain and brutality of colonization by the same people who enslaved us in the West. When those of our ancestors who were to endure the Maafa were kidnapped, they left behind their brothers, sisters, mothers, fathers, aunts, uncles, grandparents and cousins who would endure their own suffering right at home. They would live each day wondering when and if that child, husband or wife would ever return. They would spend a lifetime trying to imagine what unknown pain and horror might have befallen these loved ones. Many of them would also live to see their own enslavement in their own land in the form of European colonization, with all of the brutality and devastation it brought.

After that initial separation of the Maafa there were more to follow. Friends and relatives who were kidnapped often were placed on different ships and bound for different areas of the Western hemisphere. So even those families who where kidnapped together from Africa often went in different directions. A mother might have been sent to Brazil and her children to Cuba and North America. The father might have found himself in Jamaica , and they were never to see each other again. They would learn new languages and develop in different environments, but they remained African and family.

These were the Maafa's victims who would survive the horrible ordeals of everyday life. These brothers and sisters would persevere those traumatic circumstances only to have new families they might have formed torn apart by the sale of a child to one plantation, the sale of the mother to another, or the sale of a husband to one place and his wife to a different place. In this way Africans found themselves dispersed throughout the Western hemisphere sharing the oppression of hundreds of years as one big inseparable family, despite the breaking of immediate blood ties.

We today are the children of the sufferers and we suffer in turn. We are those who have been dispersed like so many seeds in the wind, not being sure from exactly what flower each of us has come from, but knowing we are part of a large garden that has been damaged to the point that we *must* all be family to be lifted from our oppression.

So we find ourselves now in many different places. One very effective means of keeping people oppressed is to divide and conquer. A very good example of this can be seen in the inability of Africans in America, on the level of the masses, to identify with African people the world over regardless of language, geography, class and all of the other lines that divide. One of the reasons for this is that we have largely been denied the knowledge of who we are and from where we have come. Even when there is any discussion of "slavery," it is generally dealt with superficially and as an anomaly irrelevant to the present. Unaware of our connections globally, the masses of African people, especially in America, often fail to struggle in unity with Africans worldwide. Many fail to even perceive that there is a common struggle and destiny. This has been an indirect means of keeping African people lacking in unity, by means of omission or denial of information. The major vehicle of information and socialization in our Western societies is the school system.

This school system has played a predominant role in the omission, denial and distortion of information. Through its role of socialization, it has also insured that we are perceived as "wrong" when we identify with African people worldwide. Especially in the United States, it has been stressed that we are Americans and to be consciously loyal to African people is somehow radical, anti-American, racist and militant. The other institutions in this society work in concert with the educational system to ensure that an individual's patriotism towards America cannot coexist with feelings of unity and identification with an African cultural group to end oppression. To be American is supposed to be enough and to be Pan-African/Pro-Black/anti-white supremacy/Afrocentric/cultural nationalist is unacceptable, deviant, antisocial behavior. Add to this the lack of information in the schools that draws connections between African people everywhere, and you have one component of divide and conquer. You have STIGMATIZED the African to the point where he or she, though suffering, will feel guilty about taking the necessary steps to alleviate his or her condition. That person will feel badly or "reverse racist," and be called such, when he or she joins other Africans in solidarity against the racist attitudes and institutions of America.

This is a sad state of affairs. The criminal in this case has successfully manipulated the victim into not calling the police or fighting the crime. On top of this we are much like a victim who feels that somehow it is our fault that the criminal has a gun to our head and to struggle would be doing an injustice. Again, this is divide and conquer.

Additionally, looking at the Maafa as a lesson from which to learn, one must conclude that African people have intentionally been afflicted with a lack of unity by more overt means. A speech given in 1712, by a Maafa criminal in the Caribbean named Willie Lynch, verifies the above conclusion.

Gentleman: I greet you here on the bank of the James River in the year of Our Lord one thousand seven hundred and twelve. First, I shall thank you The Gentleman of the Colony of Virginia for bringing me here. I am here to help you solve some of your problems with slaves. Your invitation reached me on my modest plantation in the West Indies where I have experimented with some of the newest and still oldest methods for control of slaves. Ancient Rome would envy us if my program is implemented. As our boat sailed south on the James River, named for our illustrious King, whose version of the Bible we cherish, I saw enough to know that your problem is not unique. While Rome used cords of wood as crosses for standing human bodies along its old highways in great numbers, you are using the tree and the rope on occasion.

I caught the whiff of a dead slave hanging from a tree a couple of miles back. You are not only losing valuable stock by hangings, you are having uprisings, slaves are running away, your crops are sometimes left in the field too long for maximum profit, you suffer occasional fires, your animals are killed, gentleman, you know what your problems are; I do not need to elaborate. I am not here to enumerate your problems, I am here to introduce you to a method of solving them.

In my bag here, I have a fool proof method for controlling Black Slaves. I guarantee everyone of you that if installed correctly, it will control the slaves for at least 300 years. My method is simple and members of your family and any Overseer can use it.

I have outlined a number of difference(s) among the slaves; and I take these differences and make them bigger. I use fear, distrust, and envy for control purposes. These methods have worked on my modest plantation in the West Indies and [they] will work throughout the South. Take this simple little list of differences, think about them. On top of my list is "Age" but it is there only because it begins with "A." The second is "Color" or "Shade," there is intelligence, size, sex, size of plantation, status of plantation, attitude of owner, whether the slaves live in the valley, on a hill, East, West, North, or South, have fine or coarse hair, or is tall or short. Now that you have a list of differences, I shall give you an outline of action but before that, I shall assure you that distrust is stronger than trust and envy is stronger than adulation, respect and admiration.

The Black Slave, after receiving this indoctrination, shall carry on and will become self-refueling and self-generating for hundreds of years, maybe thousands.

Don't forget you must pitch the old black versus the young black and the young black male against the old black male. You must use the dark skin slave vs. the light skin slaves and the light skin slaves vs. the dark skin slaves. You must also have your white servants and overseers distrust all blacks, but it is necessary that your slaves trust and depend on us. They must love, respect and trust only us.

Gentleman, these Kits are the keys to control, use them. Have your wives and children use them, never miss an opportunity. My plan is guaranteed and the good thing about this plan is that if used intensely for one year the slaves themselves will remain perpetually distrustful.

Thank you, gentleman. [1]

Beyond the obvious use of divide and conquer, there are two other lessons which should be drawn from this passage. One is that Maafa criminals communicated and cooperated in a dubious spirit of unity, but unity nonetheless. From this, one should walk away with yet another example of unity's value. The second lesson is that since these divide and conquer methods of psychological warfare were designed to keep us in a position of degradation and servitude during the Maafa and after, in examining these aspects of the Maafa we can begin to understand and remedy many of our problematic behaviors. If we believe in the problem solving logic that says in order to solve a problem you must know the cause, then we believe that we must fix what was broken in our people during the Maafa. Put more simply, if divide and conquer was used to subjugate us, we must try to reverse this process since it is the cause of the problem. In fixing what was broken, we must forge the critical links between our people that were broken as a result of forced dispersion, denial of information, miseducation, and deliberate psychological manipulation.

Essential in our endeavor to forge links between African people the world over is a more indepth understanding of the dispersion of human beings that took place during the Maafa. The great majority of Africans kidnapped came from the West Coast and Western interior regions of the vast continent. As these Africans were removed from their homeland, they were transported to different areas of the Western hemisphere. We have already described earlier how this dispersion affected families and friends.

The vast majority of Africans kidnapped during the Great Suffering went to Brazil and the Caribbean. Proportionately, a relatively small number of Africans were taken to North America. In fact, Brazil has the second largest population of African people in the world, only behind Nigeria. Caribbean islands like Jamaica, Barbados, Trinidad and Tobago, and others, are also heavily populated by Africans who are the children of the Maafa. In the preface to *Africans in Brazil*, by an African Brazilian named Abdias Do Nascimento, Dr. John Henrik Clarke shares that "Most Africans living outside of Africa are the products of the same historical events with variations depending on their respective slave masters, or colonizers." [2] In the case of Brazil it was the slavery of the Portuguese which wasn't officially outlawed until 1888, over twenty years after the proclamation ending slavery in America. Africans exist throughout South and Central America, from Argentina to Mexico.

In Central Mexico particularly, the ruthless need to kidnap Africans increased because of the decimation and elimination of millions of the Native peoples. Africans in Central Mexico "... outnumbered the Spaniards from as early as 1570. In that year, there were 14,711 Spaniards, 18,567 Black Slaves, and 1,400 mulattoes in the colony." [3]

Even in United States today the African influence in Puerto Rican culture, appearance and personality is evident. Africans who had escaped their enslavement established communities in Puerto Rico as early as 1714. Africans are also very visible in places such as Cuba, Panama, Costa Rica, Peru, Canada, Britain, etc. Beyond the language differences and cultural deviations there is little difference between Africans the world over. As Dr. Clarke wrote, we are products of the same continent and the same historical events. Thus, it should not be surprising that wherever Africans are they suffer from the common yoke of racism and oppression.

Should a body of people, forcibly removed from their homeland and dispersed around the world, allow minutia such as language to thwart alliances for the common goals of liberation and self-determination? In a sense, we African people, as children of the Maafa, are like one of the families described earlier that has been split up. Just because we have been split up, live in different areas of the world, and speak different languages doesn't make us any less related. One should ask oneself, "What is it that has made me think in such an isolated manner as to not identify with my African brothers and sisters around the world who suffer from the burden of the Maafa just as I do?" Willie Lynch's speech at the beginning of this chapter provides a partial answer to that question.

During the Maafa, especially in North America, a conscious effort was made to break ties with family, language, culture, and home-land. It was not coincidental or a mistake that Africa was shown to all people as the "dark continent" full of savages, black magic and areligious heathens. This was a process of breaking a critical identification with the Mother Continent. Once this was achieved with any degree of success (it was not completely successful as we shall see), it followed that Africans, turned "Negroes," would have a difficult time identifying and forming alliances with their fellow sufferers in the Caribbean and South America, not to mention their brothers and sisters remaining on the continent. The process of cultural degradation was so intense in North America, compared to other areas, that it is no wonder that the insurrections and rebellions in North America took a very different direction than those in other places, as we shall see later.

The connections we have with Africa and Africans can be vividly seen in several examples of communities in the Western hemisphere that have retained African cultural ties directly from Africans kidnapped during the Maafa. These communities throughout the Western hemisphere are living tributes to the resilience and survival capacity of African people. They are also a magnificent source to look to for our own identification with Mother Africa.

* * * *

Starting in North America on the Sea Islands off the coasts of South Carolina and Georgia, we can see direct links to our glorious African cultural and historical past. The children of the Maafa on these islands are most often referred to as Gullah. The term "Gullah" actually refers to the language of the Africans on the Sea Islands. The language developed out of Africans learning English and their maintaining African speech patterns and words at the same time.

Islands such as Daufuskie, Edisto, St. Helena, Sapeloe, Johns, Wadmalaw, St. Simons, and various others, represent communities of Africans who found themselves in North America as a part of the Great Suffering. Due to several factors, including many of the islands' relative isolation from the mainland and the often limited interaction of Africans with Europeans, in terms of numbers of Africans on the islands far out-numbering Europeans, islanders have retained a large degree of African cultural continuity. This is apparent in such areas as language, familial patterns, names, religion, customs, folk tales, etc.

In terms of the language, it is still very difficult to tell specific influences and contributions of various African languages and English to Gullah. In a breakdown of grammatical structure, which is one aspect of the language supposedly heavily influenced by African languages, "Gullah pronouns in All Saints Parish made no distinction between men and women. In this behavior Gullah retained a structure common to a number of African languages, such as Ibo, Ga, and Yoruba." [4] It has also been noted that

> Gullah had not one, but many African sources. Perhaps the most conspicuous was Wolof, but elements from Sierra Leone were especially important in the new language; and there were also influences from Fante, Ga, Kikongo, Kimbundu, Mandinka, Twi, Ewe, Ibo and Yoruba. [5]

Critically linked to language and African origins, are the names given to the people of these islands. In fact, although the origin of the term "Gullah" is not known for certain, it is suggested that it might come from either Angola or Gola. [6] Angola could possibly relate to Africans brought to North America from that part of Africa. Gola would refer to African groups in the area of Liberia.

As would be expected given the African influence on Gullah language,

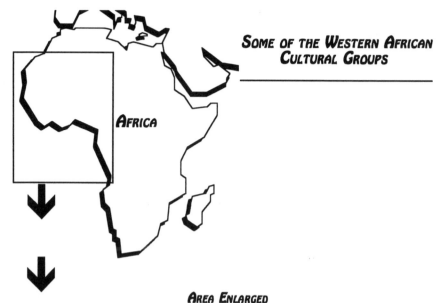

SOME OF THE WESTERN AFRICAN CULTURAL GROUPS

AFRICA

AREA ENLARGED

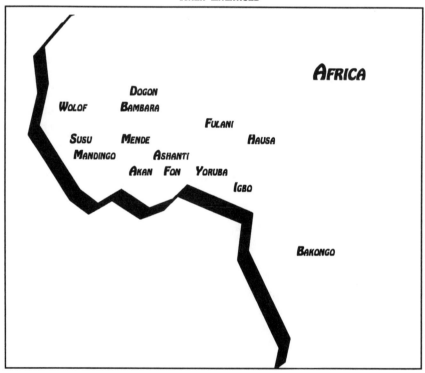

AFRICA

WOLOF
DOGON
BAMBARA
FULANI
SUSU
MENDE
HAUSA
MANDINGO
ASHANTI
AKAN FON YORUBA
IGBO
BAKONGO

The African names in Turners' listing thus indicate that among the ancestors of the Sea Islanders were speakers of a variety of languages which he identifies as Bambara, Bini, Bobangi, Djerma, Efik, Ewe, Fante, Fon, Fula, Ga, Gbari, Hausa, Ibo, Ibibio, Kikongo, Kimbundu, Kpelle, Mende, Malinke, Nupe, Susu, Songhai, Twi, Tshilubs, Umbundu, Vai, Wolof and Yoruba. The linguistic and cultural patrimony of Sea Islanders, therefore, is seen to involve an expanse of territory which includes Senegal, Gambia, Mali, Guinea, Sierra Leone, Liberia, Ivory Coast, Ghana, Togo, Benin, Niger, Nigeria, Cameroon, Equatorial Guinea, Gabon, Congo, Zaire, and Angola. [7]

One of the exciting aspects of this Sea Island culture's direct link to Africa is that there exists a more complete cultural connection than masses of Africans in America have anywhere else, given the general success of the cultural degradation and dislocation of our people during the Great Suffering.

Perhaps a most telling comment on the direct connection to Africa comes from a Sea Islander himself. He relates "I came into contact with other African students, from the continent, and had the opportunity of discussing the various customs and practices we shared. The similarities were overwhelming." [8]

The Sea Islands have a wealth of information and history to transmit, which some African scholars are attempting to tap and preserve, while leaving the communities unexploited and themselves benefiting from their wealth of historical and cultural resources. The compelling feature film by Julie Dash, *Daughters of the Dust*, has done much to bring the Sea Island Gullah culture to the front of consciousness of African people.

In Julie Dash's film we also encounter the African roots of the Gullah people. Through astonishing visual images and the actual narrative of the characters, we come face to face with their African heritage. There are particularly vivid connections to the Maafa, such as when one of the characters, Eli, walks on water to a wooden image of an enslaved African from one of the ships that brought the African ancestors to North America. At the same time that Eli is walking on water, we hear the "unborn child" narrator speaking of the ancestors who turned back and walked across the sea once they saw what was in store for them in this new place.

Along with these visual connections to the Maafa, the symbolism is very strong. Eli, who walked on water, did so after being seized or "mounted" by a spirit. This is a particularly strong inference of African religious spirituality, which we will examine later, relative to Yoruba spiritual traditions that manifest in the Western hemisphere. In the book, *Daughters of the Dust: The Making of an African American Woman's Film*, there is first hand evidence of the meaning of the symbolism in the film. In the screen play included in the book, Julie Dash's notes are hand written in the margin. Certain of her characters are meant to manifest Yoruba spirits, or orishas, through symbolism. Eli, who is seen forging iron in the film, becomes a manifestation of Ogun, the orisha of iron. Nana Peazant, who is the elder of the family, is representative of Obatala, the orisha of clarity and serenity, as well as the underlying principle or predecessor orisha. The unborn child who narrates the story is representative of Elegba, the messenger orisha who serves as the conduit between mortals and the orishas. (For more on the orishas, see chart on page 40 and a description of the orishas on page 39)

The distinct roots of Africa also surface in South America. Brazil represents a resource of African people that if only tapped can do wonders for the liberation of Africans worldwide. Brazil's retention of African culture and the spirit of resistance are models for those who seek a return to the source and real connections to that distant homeland across the Atlantic.

An intriguing area of cultural preservation is in African religion. Candomblé, Macumba, and Umbanda are three of the African Brazilian religions that were brought by Africans during the Maafa. Abdias Do Nascimento, the African Brazilian scholar and activist, perfectly illustrated the direct African connection when he wrote:

> Similar renewal of spirit came in Nigeria, where I visited Candomblé's sacred places: the ancient shrine of Oshun, where the golden fish jumped into the hands of the priest-king and founded the mythical center of her worship in Oshogbo. Although I was told that Oshun is no longer identified with art and creativity in Nigeria, her city Oshogbo is the country's most outstanding arts center, home of Twins Seven Seven and other great artists. In Ile-Ife, I saw the Ogun festival at the shrine of the cosmic warrior, shatterer of borders and barriers. I visited Oyo, historic and mythical city of Shango as well. These are African-Brazilian people's spiritual centers, our places of pilgrimage. We need no Meccas or Jerusalems. Our home in Africa is ready to receive us with our own pilgrimage points. [9]

This is powerful! This is an identification with Africa that goes deeper than any clothing, reading of books, or wearing of jewelry. It transcends the compensatory wearing of African fashions or reading of books on Africa that many Africans in the diaspora must utilize as their connection to the continent. And this is offered by one of our brothers in Brazil. The connection of Candomblé with Nigeria is due to the fact that Candomblé, as a religion, is a child of the Yoruba (of Nigeria) religion transported across the Atlantic by enslaved Africans during the Maafa. As was the case with the formation of the Gullah language of the Sea Islands, Candomblé resulted from enslaved Africans in Brazil transporting religious beliefs into the Western hemisphere and having to adjust to their captivity. This adjustment resulted in syncretism, or the blending of various aspects of different religions. In the case of Candomblé in Brazil, the Catholicism of the Portuguese enslavers met predominantly with Yoruba religion amongst the African captives. Because of this meeting and the fact that the religious practices of the kidnapped Africans had to be hidden if they weren't the selected pacifying Catholic teachings, Candomblé emerged as a disguised form of Yoruba religion, influenced by the Catholic faith. In Candomblé, the African "orishas" assume the identity of Catholic saints while maintaining their African characteristics, sometimes slightly modified in meaning and in name due to Portuguese linguistic influence. The orishas are the children and servants of "Oluddumare," God, who manifest God's will and essence. (See table on page 40) For the Catholic faith, they are similar to Saints but within an African framework of spirituality that is very different from the West. Oluddumare is one of the names for God in both Candomblé and in the parent Yoruba religion.

Although this is not a detailed examination of Candomblé, there is an obvious link to Africa manifested by our brothers and sisters in Brazil. This is especially evident in the writing of Nascimento, where the places of pilgrimage are in Africa and are as sacred as Mecca or Jerusalem. The orisha Oshun, of Candomblé, has a river so named in Oshogbo, Nigeria, one of the cities of pilgrimage in Nascimento's passage. Shango (Xangô in Brazil) and many other Yoruba orishas are also central to Candomblé.

Brazil not only has important lessons and inspiration to give to Africans everywhere, but also being a country that is majority African, has potential to impact the future of African people everywhere. With the upliftment of African people in Brazil who number some sixty million compared to America's thirty-five million, African people throughout the Diaspora and on the continent are strengthened.

Nascimento was also involved in the building of a movement in which pilgrimages are made to Serra da Berriga on National Black Consciousness Day to honor King Zumbi, who died defending the Republic of Palmares. Palmares was a free republic that resisted the onslaught of the Portuguese and Dutch in Brazil for over 100 years. (Palmares is

THE MAJOR ORISHAS

ORISHA	POWER/MANIFESTATION IN NATURE	SYMBOL
Eshu, Exu, (Legba)	messanger between divine and mortal; unpredictable; justice/crossroads	clay or cement head with facial features of cowrie shells
Obatalá, Orixalá	peace, purity, serenity, calm, clarity/fatherhood	horsetail with beaded handle
Orúnmila, Orunmilá	divination	Table of Ifá
Changó, Xangô	power, control of enemies/fire, thunder and lightening	double edged ax
Oggún, Ogum	war, employment/iron, steel	metal weapons and knives
Babalú-Ayé, Obaluaê	both cures and causes disease and illness/smallpox, leg ailments	crutches
Oshún, Oxum	love, marriage, beauty/rivers	fans, boats, mirrors
Oyá, Oiá-Iansã	protection against death/wind, burial grounds	horsetail
Yemayá, Iemanjá	maternity, womanhood/the ocean	sea shells, corals

*Yoruba spellings are not included on this chart. Forms of the orisha names represent the more popular spellings from Santería and Candomblé, in that order. Santería spellings are Spanish adaptations of Yoruba. Candomblé spellings are Portuguese adaptations of Yoruba.
**Chart is adapted from *Santería: The Religion* by Migene González-Wippler
*** Legba is voodoo.

examined in more detail later as a part of Chapter 4)

Another child of Yoruba religion is Santería, originally born in Cuba from the Africans who were kidnapped during the Great Suffering and taken there. Santería has spread throughout Latin America and the U.S. Much like Candomblé, Santería arose from syncretism and the specific circumstances of the Africans in Cuba.

Oluddumare is one of the names for God in Santería, as in Candomblé and Yoruba religion. Orishas such as Oshun, Shango (Changó in Santería) and many others are central to Santería. As Nascimento described in Candomblé, many santeros and santeras, or priests and priestesses, of Santería make journeys to Africa to learn and rediscover the origins and deeper meanings of their religion in Nigeria. [10]

Even today in North American cities such as New York, Santería is widely practiced, as is traditional Yoruba religion. Yoruba priests and priestesses can be seen in Harlem using the Yoruba term "Alafia" as a greeting and farewell and practicing their religion in temples. [11] Still other religions descended from Yoruba traditional religion surface throughout the Western hemisphere. Shango traditions are found in Trinidad and Grenada, while Kele is prevalent on St. Lucia. [12]

New Orleans provides another well known but severely maligned and misunderstood manifestation of a direct link to Africa. The West African, specifically Dahomean, religion of Vodu has become widely known to most Americans as voodoo and commonly associated with New Orleans. The misunderstanding of the religion of voodoo, as well as its African origins, are clearly expressed in the following passage.

> The word voodoo, which is Dahomean in origin and means
> "spirit" or "deity" in the Fon language, generally produces one of three
> responses from most Westerners: fear, laughter, or respect. The
> response of fear is based on exaggerated negative views of the super-
> natural world and of Africa. The laughter response is often motivated
> by an ignorance that associates voodoo with "mere superstition."
> Respect comes with one's knowledge that voodoo is a functional
> religious system in West Africa. [13]

Yet another vivid example of connections to the Motherland are our brothers and sisters in Jamaica who call themselves Rastafarians. They show an overt and conscious linkage to Africa in their reverence for Haile Selaisse, former Emperor of Ethiopia. Haile Selassie's name, prior to taking the name Haile Selassie upon his coronation to emperor, was Ras Tafari. Hence, the name Rastafarian. The popular phrase, known to many non-Rastas, of "Jah-Ras-Tafari" refers to the former emperor in divine reverence by the addition of "Jah" which means God. Haile Selassie linked his line of descent to the Biblical King Solomon and is viewed by Rastafarians as the African Messiah returned to redeem Africans exiled throughout the world as a result of the Great Suffering.

Ethiopia is seen as the promised land. The African character of the Rastafarian religion is voiced forthrightly by Rastas. This character or spirit of the Motherland is also apparent in the name of one of the most important meetings or periodic gatherings of the Rastafarians, known as Nyabingi. Nyabingi is a term which is thought to come form East Africa and is possibly the name or title of an African sister who resisted colonial domination. [14] The African term, Nyabingi, also is directly linked to another important aspect of Rastafarianism, which is resistance to oppression.

Artists like Bob Marley wrote songs like *Africa Unite, Zimbabwe*, and referred to oppressors "sucking the blood of the sufferers." In fact, Marley had a *tremendous* amount of socio-political insight in his music. Bob Marley was a Rastafarian who personified resistance and Rastafarianism on the world stage.

Although Rastafarianism is the most popular Jamaican image, older and more direct links to African victims of the Great Suffering exist. Another religion practiced in Jamaica is Kumina, which is of Ashanti origin and was carried from Africa by victims of the Great Suffering. The word, Kumina, comes from the Twi language of the Ashanti and means to be possessed by an ancestor. [15] Even today "the language of Jamaican peasants still carries hundreds of words that need no translation from the original Ashanti tongue- Twi." [16]

All of the above examples of African culture, especially religion given its dominant cultural role, surviving throughout the Diaspora and descending directly from Africans during the Maafa, are for the sole purpose of showing the global connections of African people. Despite the predominant focus here on religion, one who travels throughout the Diaspora can see the many manifestations of African connections in art, language, dress and many other areas. Whether in Jamaica, the Bahamas, or other Caribbean islands, one can pick up African wood carvings, canes, baskets, etc. Though much misinformation and purposeful psychological manipulation has made many of us ignorant of our connections with the "majority" of African people and other people of color around the world, we must realize that our destinies and identities are *inseparable* from African people wherever they may be. This realization can only lead to unity, which was proven earlier to be an essential component toward freedom.

Unity is a point of departure for African people in terms of shaping our own destinies, as any and every people must do. This knowledge of our connections with the African continent and African people also corrects "the abduction and unhealthy educational enslavement of African-Americans." [17] We can grow in our identification and linkage to a past and homeland, which is essential for our grounding in a hostile place of exile. We gain a perspective of our existence in place and time as it relates to the rest of the world, which is empowering in itself. As Africans in America witness and enjoy a surge in African philosophy, dress, and resistance, we must remember that it is all superficial and useless if it doesn't allow us to identify with Africans on the continent and around the world, the majority of whom fight the same struggles as we do.

CHAPTER 4

RESISTANCE THAT HAS ALLOWED US TO EXIST

* King Zumbi, Republic of Palmares, Pernambuco, Brazil 1605-1694 (1st Republic in Western hemisphere. Africans fought the Maafa by establishing their own nation.)

* Africans in Suriname revolt and wage war on their oppressors for over 200 years. Six "Maroon" tribes exist to this day and still struggle, despite many winning freedom in 1762.

Revolution	Revolts
* Boukman	*** Gabriel Prosser**, Virginia,1800
Toussaint L'Ouverture	*** Sancho**, Virginia,1802
Jean Jaques Dessalines	*** Denmark Vesey**, South Carolina 1822
Henri Christophe	*** Nat Turner**, Virginia 1831
leaders of the **Haitian**	*** Stono Rebellion**, South Carolina 1739
Revolution, 1791-1804	

* Seminole Nation (African/Native American Alliance), 1776-1858. Waged war against U.S.

* Africans navigate return home to the Motherland after overtaking their ship of enslavement, the *Little George*, in 1730. 9 day return trip.

* Africans return home after taking over their ship of enslavement, the *William,* from the control of their kidnappers in 1732.

* Africans on the *Creole* take over the ship bound for New Orleans from Hampton, Va. and sail to the Bahamas in 1841.

* Joseph Cinque led	*** Ñanga(Yanga)** lead the settlement of free Africans in
Amistad mutiny at sea, 1841.	Central Mexico

* Cudjoe	*** Domingo Bioho (King Benkos)**
Accompong	Leader of revolt in Colombia
Cofi (Cuffee)	
Quaco	
Johnny	
Acheampong Nanny	

were all leaders of **Jamaican Maroons**, late 1600's and 1700's

The previous list of only a few of the many heroic efforts of Africans suffering through the Maafa gives an idea of the degree of strength and perseverance that violently shook the foundations of the Maafa and those perpetrating this horrible event in time.

Throughout the Western hemisphere, African resistance made the perpetuation of the Great Suffering a dangerous and frightening venture of immorality for Europeans. In fact, the revolutions, revolts and rebellions waged by enslaved Africans did more than is admitted in today's history books to end the physical enslavement of the Great Suffering. Africans, regardless of where they existed, engaged in constant and relentless struggle and warfare. From the coast of Africa to the Atlantic Ocean; from Haiti to Virginia and South Carolina; from Brazil to Jamaica, Suriname, Colombia, Central Mexico, Venezuela, St. Lucia, Cuba and anywhere else African people suffered, there was resistance and revolution.

This is an important legacy and one that African people should become aware of and find comfort in. Just as European Americans celebrate the American Revolution and Independence Day, Africans should hold our history of struggle in reverence and pride. Our heros and heroines are not only the great African kings and queens of old. Nor are our heroic figures confined to the Malcolm Xs and Martin Luther Kings, but they must include Maafa warriors like Denmark Vesey, Nat Turner, Gabriel Prosser, our sister Acheampong Nanny, Dessalines, L'Ouverture, Queen Nzinga, Boukman, King Zumbi and many others.

These brothers and sisters represented the sane and brave Africans in the madness of war, enslavement and brutality. It is sane and noble to fight against the death of oneself and one's people, represented by the Great Suffering. Given this history of self-defense and self-determination, there is no shame in the Maafa for Africans. Currently, this information and history of resistance is largely denied and omitted from history books, while being countered by the image of the docile enslaved African. History texts of the United States educational system romanticize the Great Suffering when it is covered to any significant degree, while presenting students with text that says "Some slaves even attacked their masters or organized slave revolts like the one led by Nat Turner. But these revolts had little chance of succeeding." [1] This quote, from a widely used and respected Social Studies series, sadly underplays the importance and impact of resistance, while comprising the majority of what is even mentioned about resistance in the text.

It is estimated that over 150 rebellions took place at sea during the Middle Passage and in the Western hemisphere Africans rose in over 250 instances of determined resistance. And, as we shall see, these were significant events that shook the world and not mere trifles of enslaved Africans "with little chance of success." Consistent with our precise use of language, we would be well served to approach these subjects of resistance by their character as revolution, nation building or revolt/rebellion/insurrection.

A revolution is defined as "The overthrow of one government and its replacement with another." [2] A separate class of resistance will be referred to as nation building, where Africans collectively established their own nations or societies rather than moving solely to overthrow existing Maafa criminals. Finally, revolts/rebellions/insurrections are terms that are basically synonymous and defined generally as attempts to overthrow governments or opposition to something. The inference in this third category of resistance is that a revolt/rebellion/insurrection is not successful, since it is an *attempt* to overthrow, whereas the revolution *is* the overthrow of government and its replacement, indicating success. Nation building is also marked by success since it accomplishes the end aims of revolution which essentially involve change and self-determination. Looking at resistance in these categories will help us understand and question the nature of the events which fit into them.

❖ Nation Building ❖

The Republic of Palmares in Brazil, established by Africans in 1605 and consisting of Africans and Native peoples, was the first republic or nation with territorial and political autonomy in the Western hemisphere outside of the Native American nations that existed before being annihilated. The United States was the second republic.

Palmares, under the leadership of King Zumbi, established a republic and defended it successfully against the Portuguese and the Dutch from 1605-1694. Africans who had escaped enslavement populated Palmares and lived in an organized and independent society. The profound impact of this historical success against the Maafa is seen today in the fact that African Brazilians celebrate Zumbi and embark on pilgrimages to Palmares as a liberation rallying point.

Societies established by Africans who liberated themselves from bondage have been known by various names given their proliferation in various geographic regions of the Western hemisphere. *Mocambo* and *Quilombo* in Brazil, *Cumbe* in Venezuela, *Palenque* in Cuba, Mexico, etc., and Maroon societies in the English speaking world, all describe communities of Africans who had liberated themselves and began the task of nation building. Part of this nation building involved defense and the waging of war against aggressive Maafa criminals such as the Portuguese and Dutch in Brazil.

The Matawai, Saramacca, Kwinti, Djuka, Paramaka and Aluka are all Surinamese Maroon communities that still exist today as descendants of the original Africans who liberated themselves. Suriname is a South American country just above Brazil and bordering the Caribbean, which is the home of the longest surviving autonomous Maroon societies. Surinamese maroons engaged in wars of liberation that lasted over 50 years, before many of these groups signed treaties with the Dutch in the 1760's.

In Jamaica there is also a history of resistance by Maroon societies formed in the hills of that country. These Africans engaged in guerilla warfare with the British for over one hundred years.

In 1655, the Spanish, who were previously the colonial invaders of Jamaica, were overtaken by the British. The problems of the British began immediately as the Africans already in the hills were joined by Africans who took advantage of the change of colonial occupation from Spain to Britain. It is safe to say that the British may have seen the Maroons as more of a threat and concern than the Spanish were at the time.

Some of the well known Maroon leaders, thought to be Akan Africans, are Cudjoe, Accompong, Cofi (Cuffee), Johnny and Acheampong Nanny. Nanny was a woman who led the resistance and is a well known figure in Jamaica. There are said to have been many other African women who fought and held positions of leadership, but history has not passed their names down to us.

These Africans found a way to resist the Maafa and live for themselves, sustaining agricultural production and trade in market places. The British were forced to sign peace treaties (as decietful as we know these to be) with the Maroons because their resistance was so fierce and damaging to the forces of Britain.

❖ Revolution ❖

Perhaps the best known event of resistance is the Haitian Revolution, involving such well known personalities as Touissaint L'Ouverture and Jean Jacques Dessalines. In the summer of 1791, what was then known as San Domingo was on the verge of revolution. On one particular evening the African drums are said to have summoned enslaved

African leaders to the hills for a secret meeting with a priest of voodoo named Boukman; and this was the genesis of revolution. Freedom or death was the vow and "Eight days later-- at midnight on August 22, 1791 -- one hundred thousand slaves answered with a revolution..." [3]

Plantations were set ablaze and reciprocity visited Maafa criminals and snatched life wherever it ventured. This beginning set the stage for the entrance of a profound military mind and African hero, Francois Dominique Toussaint L'Ouverture. Toussaint trained and organized an army of Africans that outsmarted and outfought armies from Spain, France and Britain. After Toussaint L'Ouverture, Jean Jaques Dessalines and Henri Christophe continued the leadership of the revolution which ended in November 1803 with the surrender of Napoleon's French forces and the establishment of the Republic of Haiti, complete with its declaration of independence, in 1804.

This is a powerful example of resistance that shows Africans handily defeating Western world powers. The example of determination and heroic action embodied in the Haitian Revolution can only empower African people, even today after 191 years.

❖ Revolts/Rebellions/Insurrections ❖

Just because this category of resistance by definition infers a lack of success regarding liberation, this is not to say that the revolts dealt with here were poorly planned or stood little chance of succeeding. To the contrary, we will see that many revolts were meticulously planned and, if not for some twist of fate or misfortune, might well have been the beginnings of revolution. This insight is important, especially for Africans in America where revolution did not take place, but significant and well planned revolts could well have been the beginnings of revolution in North America. One need only imagine the implications an African revolution might have had on the present day United States in general, and African people in particular.

In the year 1800, a man named Gabriel Prosser shook America with a plan to take the city of Richmond and liberate Africans in Virginia by quick strikes on other Virginia cities after Richmond was secured. Gabriel's rebellion was not an isolated event, but part of a continuum of resistance. Gabriel was aware of what had taken place in Haiti and drew inspiration from Toussaint L'Ouverture.

Gabriel Prosser's plan involved three groups, or militarily organized columns, of Africans attacking Richmond. One of those columns would attack the armory and seize weapons while capturing Governor James Monroe in the nearby Governor's mansion. The second and third columns of Africans would set diversionary fires and take control of bridges, while fortifying the city. This plan had enlisted "several thousand" Africans after months of planning and recruiting. [4] The revolution was scheduled for midnight August 30th. It can be rightfully called a revolution at this point, because the object was governmental overthrow, plans of military attack were in place and weapons were assembled with plans to secure more. The revolution in genesis became a revolt when two Africans sold out and told their masters of the plan. This act of treason, and inclement weather classified the impending revolution as a revolt/rebellion/insurrection before it began, because Gabriel was captured and, along with many fellow revolutionaries, tried before being hung. The date of the hanging, October 7, 1800, should be a day of remembrance for African people. August 30th, the scheduled date of revolution's beginnings, should be a day of intense reflection on true freedom for all Africans and a special day in the continuous struggle of conscious Africans.

In 1822, an African named Denmark Vesey of Charleston, South Carolina, heard the voice of Toussaint L'Ouverture and was known to frequently quote him. Vesey planned revolution. Scheduled for July 16, 1822, Charleston was to come under attack by an African army estimated to have been a recruited body that would have consisted of 9,000 men. Secret meetings and the recruiting efforts of men like Mingo Hearth and Peter Poyas allowed for a well organized and workable plan of simultaneous attack on arsenals, guard houses, naval stores and other strategic points.

Like Prosser, Vesey's revolutionary plans turned into simply a revolt when they were sold out by fellow Africans who had been sufficiently conditioned to love the slavemaster more than their own brothers and sisters struggling for the freedom of all. Vesey was hung on July 2, 1822. This date should be one of remembrance and July 16 should be the day of mass reflection.

One of the best known names of any enslaved African, outside of the fictional Kunta Kente, is that of Nat Turner. In 1831, Nat Turner was able to execute his rebellion. Far short of the recruited thousands of Vesey and Prosser, Turner embarked on a mission of personal conviction and passion, along with seven other men. On the night of August 21, 1831, Nat Turner led reciprocity on a visit through Southampton County, Virginia, picking up recruits along the way as they left over fifty casualties in their wake. However, even with those they picked up along the way, Nat Turner and his crew of warriors were no more than seventy in number. This small group fought but eventually was overwhelmed. Nat Turner was not captured for weeks. Finally he was captured and eventually hung on November 11, 1831, a day on which we should remember.

★ ★ ★ ★

The above mentioned revolts/rebellions/insurrections are only three of hundreds that occurred in the U.S. and throughout the Western hemisphere. Other revolts occurred in Brazil, Honduras, Costa Rica, Cuba, Peru, Mexico, Panama, Barbados, Jamaica, Suriname, St. Lucia, New York City, Florida and anywhere else Africans endured the Great Suffering.

On the continent of Africa, Maafa ships of enslavement were sometimes overpowered by fellow Africans coming to the rescue of their brothers and sisters. Queen Nzinga gives us the best known example of this resistance. Queen Nzinga was from the region of Africa recognized as Angola and was described as one of the greatest military strategists to ever do battle with the Portuguese. If their can be identified a predecessor to the Black Liberation Army of the sixties and seventies in America, Queen Nzinga's army might be it. She fought relentlessly against the Maafa criminals and was such a profound strategist that she confused the Portuguese and instilled fear in their numbers. According to Chancellor Williams in *The Destruction of Black Civilization*, Nzinga waged war for forty years until she passed away.

At sea, Africans made the phrase "freedom or death" ring true in successful overthrows of ship's crews and returns to Africa, as well as taking their own lives or the lives of children rather than endure the Great Suffering.

If an analogy may be applied to resistance during the Maafa, psychologically speaking, if a child were to be separated from his or her parents, the child would want to know that his or her parents fought for that child. If the child believes the parents failed to fight, there could be a negative impression left on the child. The child might have anger, resentment, dislike and strong impressions of the worthlessness of such parents. Consequently, the parent-child biological and social association might lead the child to negative conscious or subconscious feelings about him or herself. Thus, the child might act out these negative concepts of self in various ways.

It is not extraordinary to believe that for those Africans who have bought in to the stories of the docility of their forebears and their

51

acceptance of enslavement, much like the child negative feelings towards these ancestors might prevail. They may feel negatively towards these Africans they see as failing to fight the Maafa, beyond running away and getting a foot chopped off or being whipped. These same negative feelings may render their possessors, African descendants, guilty by association so that they feel conscious or subconscious shame and anger towards who and what they are, as well as from where they have come. In other words, being the sons and daughters of Africans perceived as failing to fight the Maafa, many have feelings of self-hatred that manifests in "Black on Black" crime, inactivity towards getting out of their own oppressive situations and feelings of inferiority.

On the other hand, the knowledge that parents or ancestors were strong and fought can be a source of pride and inspiration. Further, when one becomes aware of the resistance of Africans wherever they were in the Western hemisphere it is perhaps easier to conceptualize unified, global, continuous struggle for liberation. One has an easier time learning to love oneself, making the willingness to inflict pain and death on those like them, "Black on Black crime," far less likely. There is also the realization that inferior conditions require resistance and change.

What is hoped for here is the positive psychological and tactical effect of knowing the resistance of our ancestors, as well as the historical framework for action that we might adopt to our time and circumstances, in the spirit of unity.

With these thoughts in my mind we would be remiss in not considering at least a few of the Africans who lifted their *voices* and dedicated themselves to resistance. Most are familiar with Frederick Douglass, an escaped slave himself, who eloquently asserted that:

> If there is no struggle, there is no progress.... This struggle
> may be a moral one, or it may be a physical one, and it may be both
> moral and physical, but it must be a struggle. Power concedes nothing
> without demand. [5]

We are also quite accustomed to hearing the name of Harriet Tubman and that of Sojourner Truth. These sisters certainly serve notice to men that we are foolish if we do not recognize the vast importance of women, not simply in the sexist "stand by your man" mentality, but in their resistance, leadership and ability to stand in front of men.

These popular names are familiar to us, but respect and love is also due to the likes of David Walker and Henry Highland Garnet. Each of these men spoke uncompromisingly about the need for the African to resist enslavement.

David Walker in his *Walker's Appeal, in Four Articles: Together With a Preamble, to the Coloured Citizen of the World, and Very Expressly, to Those of the United States of America.*, expressed his revolutionary spirit, saying:

> Now, I ask you, had you not rather be killed than to be a slave to a tyrant, who takes the life of your mother, wife, and dear little children? Look upon your mother, wife, and children, and answer God Almighty; and believe this, that it is no more harm for you to kill a man, who is trying to kill you, than it is for you to take a drink of water when thirsty; in fact, the man who will stand still and let another murder him, is worse than an infidel, and, if he has common sense, ought not to be pitied... [6]

Henry Highland Garnet affirmed this revolutionary spirit in his "Address to the Slaves of the United States." Garnet's fire proclaimed that:

> You had better all die--die immediately, than live slaves and entail your wretchedness upon your posterity... However much you and all of us may desire it, there is not much hope of redemption without the shedding of blood. [7]

David Walker, born in 1785, wrote his *Appeal* in 1829. He died the year after publishing his *Appeal*, by what is considered foul play. Henry Highland Garnet was born in 1815 and delivered his famous speech in 1843.

Ida B. Wells is another of our sisters who stepped to the forefront of struggle. Born in 1862 while the Maafa was still an official practice in North America and not yet near the end in Brazil, Wells stepped forward most notably in her speeches and publication protesting the lynching of African people. Her publication, *The Red Record*, was a statistical compilation of the record on lynching. This sister, who passed away in 1931, was a champion for her people.

Martin R. Delaney was born in 1812 and was the grandson of Africans brought directly from the continent. This African brother came forth as a staunch "Black Nationalist." His stance on self-determination and   independence for African people would influence those to follow him, as would his pride in being an African. Delaney self-published *The Condition, Elevation, Emigration and Destiny of the Colored People of the United States, Politically Considered.*

It is no wonder that men and women such as these are not subjects concentrated upon in America's history texts. They are not palatable to America. The descendants of the Maafa criminals who have any power, control, or wealth, benefit directly from the Maafa and its legacy; they have no longing to see today's inactive, pacified, and sleeping masses of Africans slapped into action, consciousness, and resistance by the words of those like Walker and Garnet.

There are countless others who deserve our recognition, respect and study. In more recent years people like the Honorable Marcus Mosiah Garvey and the Honorable Elijah Muhammed are neglected. These warriors and others will be dealt with in the portion of this work dedicated to the Maafa Aftermath (the time from so called emancipation on into the present predicament).

PART II
THE AFTERMATH: BEYOND THE MAAFA

CHAPTER 5

A LEGACY OF CONTINUED STRUGGLE

The end of the Great Suffering did not end the suffering of African people. The Great Suffering, which consumed hundreds of years and millions of lives, had extensive repercussions for African people. One can take a rudimentary look at these repercussions by categorizing the long term effects of the Great Suffering as those that affected the Africans on the continent and those that affected Africans taken to the Western hemisphere. It must be kept in mind, however, that events taking place in each place integrally affected Africans everywhere.

❖ Africa ❖

Much of the debate taking place in the Western academic world, concerning the Maafa and the numbers of African victims, is due to current attempts to gage the long term effects of the Maafa on subsequent European colonization of Africa and the continent's underdevelopment. Naturally, the massive depopulation of the African continent resulting from the Maafa is a part of the consideration, thus the recent flurry in debate (discussed in the first chapter) over how many millions of Africans were lost. The current and continuous instability of Africa, politically and economically, is tied to this history of enslavement and colonization. Therefore, how the history of colonization and enslavement is interpreted takes on political, social and economic significance for today's policy interpretation and administration. This history is thus prime for European hegemonic interpretation, but there are those who will no longer allow history to be "whitewashed."

The obvious connection of the Maafa to colonization is argued by Joseph Inikori.

Our central argument is that between 1450 and 1870, export demand for captives kept the total population of Tropical Africa at a level that was far too low to stimulate a widespread development of the division of labour, the growth of internal trade, diversification of the economy, transformation of technology and organization of production, and class differentiation. At the same time, export for captives retarded the development of commodity production for export, with similar consequences... Ultimately, these factors acted together as a chain on Tropical African societies in their movement toward sociopolitical and economic transformation. This situation facilitated the imposition of European colonial domination, which aggravated the problem structurally, technologically and mentally-- in this way, hardening the chain. [1]

The editor of a new volume entitled *The African Slave Trade*, further verifies the connection when he writes that "Finally, the Atlantic Slave Trade has been seen not only as affecting Africa during the four centuries of its existence but also leading to the later European takeover of the continent and causing its present-day underdevelopment." [2]

It is paramount that we as African people make the "critical-thinking" connections that allow us to interpret what is taking place in Africa as it relates to us and African people everywhere. Whether we realize it or not, we are inextricably linked to the fate of Africa. Too many of us have a pitiful understanding of our homeland and consequently are capable of doing little if anything to support Africa as a strong U. S. lobby (the way the Jewish community impacts U.S. foreign policy and funding of Israel or the way politicized Cuban communities influence U.S. policy towards Cuba and Castro). We also fail to share and utilize one another's resources on a mass level, whether those resources be people, land, money, agricultural, etc. Given these realities it is hoped that this book in general, and this section in particular, will help more of us along the road of empowerment and politicized understanding of our current situation as African people.

****

Though the European colonization and rape of Africa was and is a complex process rather than a single event, The Berlin West African Conference can be viewed as a key point in time regarding the European assault on Africa. It is true that Europeans were meddling in Africa centuries before and had substantial criminal exploits there resulting from the Maafa, but from November 1884 to February 1885 the Berlin Conference "established the rule that henceforth 'effective occupation' was to be the sole valid title to African coastal territory." [3] In other words, to avoid all out conflict and war between the greedy European powers scrambling for Africa, ground rules were established for this scramble which stated that you've got to be there and in control to call it yours. This meant no more of the British practice of simply claiming parts of Africa as part of an Empire.

> Participants in the Berlin Conference of 1884-5 hoped that, by prescribing a code of behaviour for foreigners seeking to control the coasts and rivers which gave access to African commerce, they had established their own imperial responsibilities. The new proce- dures for partition of the littoral regulated a process of scrambling for protectorates which was already almost complete; by 1855 only the stretch between the Mano river and France's outposts on the Ivory Coast remained unclaimed by Europeans. [4]

Bismarck of Germany organized the conference, and from that point Europeans made deals and signed treaties with other Europeans securing their "rights" to pieces of the African continent. It was organized and they were unified on at least one point; they wanted the resources and money to be made in Africa and they needed to be united to some degree to achieve this.

Leopold of Belgium moved aggressively on the central area of Africa which became known as the Belgian Congo and is now Zaire. Bismarck's Germany moved on Togo; they moved on what was then Kamerun and is now Cameroon; former South West Africa, now Namibia; Ruanda-Urundi, now Rwanda and Burundi; and Tanganyika, now known as Tanzania. Bismarck acted out much of this criminal aggression before the Berlin Conference and then organized the conference to set the rules.

Britain acted out criminal aggression and greed on the Sudan; Uganda, as a protectorate in 1895; Kenya in 1895; the Island of Zanzibar in 1890 as a protectorate; Malawi in 1891; Southern Rhodesia, now Zimbabwe; Northern Rhodesia, now Zambia; Botswana, Gambia, Sierra Leone and Nigeria. The French took the former Soudan, now Mali; what is now Benin, formerly Dahomey; Niger, Mauritania, Morocco, Cote D'Ivoire, Gabon, Central African Republic, and Chad. The French had already exercised some degree of control on Algeria and Tunisia in North Africa. Italy was defeated by the Ethiopians, but came back over thirty years later in 1935 and annexed Ethiopia. Italy also exploited and controlled Eritrea and Somalia. The Portuguese, not to be left out, had Angola and Mozambique, with designs on Madagascar, but the French were also interested and proclaimed it theirs. The Portuguese also had control in Guinea, now Guinea -Bassau, Cape Verde, and the islands of Sao Tome and Principe. Spain exploited Rio Muni, now Equatorial Guinea. America invested in the money making exploitation throughout the continent, including the slavery in South Africa.

The question we should be asking is "What gives Europeans the right to do these things?" They arrived in North America and received the acceptance and friendship of Native Americans only to pay them back with ruthless, barbaric annihilation. We have just discussed what they have done to Africa. A recurring theme in history has been the European tendency to act out the most anti-human, aggressive, violent behavior of any group of people in the world. They have shown the ability to justify and feel comfortable taking what is not theirs at the cost of millions of human lives. If we are to learn from the history of colonization and other sordid episodes of the European past, we should learn that welcoming anyone with open, unquestioning arms is not an intelligent thing to do. This applies especially to welcoming Europeans. We as an African people need to WAKE UP.

These European powers, of course, did not simply walk into Africa and say, "this is mine." There was much resistance, revolution and rebellion. Unfortunately, the onslaught was so concerted, organized, malicious and greed driven that Africa was consumed. However, as we Africans in America earned the right to be *called* free, Africa did the same. Names like Kwame Nkrumah of Ghana, Julius Nyere in Tanganyika, Patrice Lumumba in the Congo, Jomo Kenyatta and the Mau Mau revolt in 1950's Kenya, Nelson and Winnie Mandela, Steven Biko, Tom Mboya, Chris Hani, Amilcar Cabral and many other people and organizations speak volumes of resistance. The independence dates of African countries are as follows:

Libya, 1951	Cote d'Ivoire, 1960	Gambia, 1965
Sudan, 1956	Chad, 1960	Botswana, 1966
Morocco, 1956	The Central African Republic, 1960	Lesotho, 1966
Tunisia, 1956	The Congo, 1960	Mauritius, 1968
Ghana, 1957	Gabon, 1960	Swaziland, 1968

A Legacy of Continued Struggle

Guinea, 1958	Nigeria, 1960	Equatorial Guinea, 1968
Cameroon, 1960	Mauritania, 1960	Guinea Bassau, 1974
Togo, 1960	Sierra Leone, 1961	Mozambique, 1975
Mali, 1960	Tanzania, 1961	Cape Verde, 1975
Senegal, 1960	Rwanda, 1962	The Comoros, 1975
Madagascar, 1960	Burundi, 1962	Sao Tome an Principe, 1975
Zaire, 1960	Algeria, 1962	Angola, 1975
Somalia, 1960	Uganda, 1962	Seychelles, 1976
Benin, 1960	Kenya, 1963	Djibouti, 1977
Niger, 1960	Malawi, 1964	Zimbabwe, 1980
Burkina Faso, 1960	Zambia, 1964	Namibia, 1990

Eritrea, 1993   South Africa, 1994

Even with this independence movement, we must realize certain things. First of all, just as Africans in America gained "so called" freedom with emancipation, much of Africa's independence is "so called" independence. Many of these African countries remain dependent economically, structurally and educationally on Europe. Just like in America, there came a time when resistance was too fierce and, put bluntly, slavery and colonialism in their existing forms were no longer necessary for Europeans. In America, the economy, major institutions, real political control, and our minds through education, are still controlled by European Americans for many of us. In Africa, the same situations existed and exist. Therefore, the physical chains were no longer necessary in either situation.

Chancellor Williams, as one of our esteemed ancestors, was wise and profoundly insightful, not only in his well known book, *The Destruction of Black Civilization*, but also in *The Rebirth of African Civilization*. He spoke directly to the African condition in independence.

> And in no area will any nation find the call for the greatest emphasis, faster pace, and unprecedented scope more urgent than in the field of education. Sound government and wise political action rest squarely on it. Economic development of Africa *by Africans* depends directly on it. [5]

Williams also went on to ask the critical question of what we mean by education. He knew it couldn't be the system of the former colonizer, because that system was designed for failure, dependency and self-hatred. He stated clearly as early as 1961 that:

> Fortunately, Africans know that they must develop their own educational institutions. British Africa cannot remain British; French Africa cannot remain French; Belgian and Portuguese Africa cannot remain Belgian and Portuguese. We might as well expect the Africans of South Africa to accept the Boer philosophy when they become free-- and they will become free. [6]

This declaration by Williams includes Africans who run educational systems on the same philosophical basis as those who oppressed them. There are many of us here in America and on the continent who think culturally and philosophically more European than Europeans. An African face cannot simply take the place of a European face. A shift in consciousness and ideology is also necessary, which has been lacking in many of those who have assumed leadership positions. Therefore, an

African face replaces a Belgian one, but the institution remains Belgian in character and ideology. This simply will not do. Dark skin and African features are not all that is required to be a champion and ally of African people. This not only applies to Africa, but also to many of the so called leaders who have been designated by Europeans to be our spokespeople in the United States. When it comes down to it, the only acceptable situation is African people handling their own business wherever they are in the world. And, this business must be handled by those whose interests represent the best interests of African people, period! This is nothing to ask and is in no way out of the ordinary. America as an example; you will never find Europeans allowing Africans or anyone else to run their affairs. There will be no Africans determining what the policy and direction of the Anti-Defamation League (ADL) of B'nai B'rith will be. You will never see Jewish people appointing an African person, or people, to run the affairs of the ADL or any other European Jewish organization. That is precisely how it should and must be, especially in today's world. It would be abnormal and contradictory for it to be any other way. Likewise, it can no longer be considered normal for people outside of the African community to run and participate in our every organization. There are certain things that a family must take care of between family members only. If you are not part of the family it is none of your business. The same applies with the family of African people. It is equally unacceptable for the Africans who run our organizations and institutions to be ONLY those deemed acceptable by people other than Africans.

So, the question at this point might be, "why Africa?" "Why the wholesale and organized assault on Africa and her people?" In answering these questions it should be remembered that Africa is one of the richest continents in the world with regard to resources. Dubois mentioned, in *The World and Africa*, that "out of Africa come 95 per cent of the world's diamonds; 80 per cent of the cobalt; 60 per cent of the Gold... " [7] and the list goes on. Dubois was writing around the middle of this century. The updated figures still support the mineral richness of Africa, with the rest of the world's minerals and premium crops coming predominately out of places like South America and Australia, not the U.S. or Europe. From Cassava to chromium, from Cocoa beans to Uranium and uncut diamonds, Africa supplies a large portion of the West's resources. The sad part is that many of the minerals being mined in African countries and warehoused in Europe are non-replenishable. These minerals are exploited to the point that some African countries that supplied extremely high percentages of particular resources to the world twenty years ago, now supply much smaller percentages based on the fact that they are being drained dry.

Given the richness of the African continent, one is forced to question why masses of Africans languish in poverty and famine? Why does one of the richest, resource filled continents on the planet constantly surface in Western circles as needing population control to avoid an ecological catastrophe and ensure the health/prosperity of its people? The answer lies in colonization and the continued economic and resource exploitation by Europe. Africa could sustain her people without problems if her resources and profitability were being used at home instead of in gross excess in "so called" developed countries, leaving the African masses the targets of population control imposed by the "World Community."

To the economic exploitation of the West, add racism and white world supremacy and you have the beginnings of a clear view of the historical continuum that includes and connects the Maafa, European colonization of Africa, and Africa's present turmoil and dependence on the World Bank and International Monetary Fund, who give conditions of structural change favorable to the West before lending money and placing countries deep in debt.

Whenever images are seen today of corrupt regimes and ethnic strife in Africa, the intelligent person must ask "what European country is behind the corrupt government, funding dictators or creating instability with international 'intelligence agencies?'" Also, before colonization in Africa most of the countries, their borders, and the forced intermingling of culturally different groups did not exist. This was the expedient planning of Europe, but an unnatural, artificially produced social structure for Africa. This is a contributing factor when it comes to ethnic strife, along with the fact that European colonizers consciously and admittedly created ethnic strife and division where there was none beyond the ordinary differences and conflicts that exist between peoples no matter who or where they are in the world. It is that common tactic called divide and conquer.

Even with all of this, we can excuse neither ourselves nor our African brothers and sisters on the continent when immoral and self-destructive behaviors exist. Self-examination is a necessity. However, we must be able to critically analyze what is taking place on the continent and become politically astute directors and protectors of the policies directed towards our homeland that affect us all. We must also become active and progressive enough to participate in the dynamic changes taking place in Africa. By being there, doing business there without exploiting, building up Africa and being rejuvenated by positive alliances with Africans on the continent that help us build throughout the Western hemisphere, we can begin to accomplish this.

❖ Western Hemisphere ❖

Many of us are a little more familiar with what has taken place here in America beyond the Maafa. With the "so called" emancipation came the formation of the Ku Klux Klan and other oppressive groups to ensure a new kind of slavery and terror; followed shortly thereafter by the Jim Crow era just before the turn of the century. Jim Crow took us from the late 1800's on up to the 50's and 60's Civil Rights movement. So in terms of chronology, we were called free in 1863, assaulted at every turn as soon as we were free and returned to a different face of legal slavery called Jim Crow in the 1890's. We were still fighting for rights only thirty years ago in the Civil Rights movement, and now in 1995 we still see rampant discrimination, inequity, negative images, hostility and the masses receiving inadequate and inappropriate education from their former slave masters.

It is significant for African people to reflect and realize that we are only thirty years removed from legal discrimination. One must comprehend the fact that this means those African people under thirty years of age are the first generation to be born with at least the illusion of equality in this country. This is a very short period of time! How much could negative attitudes, entrenched for hundreds of years, change with the simple movement of a pen across a piece of legislation? The truth is that with the "official" end of the Maafa in 1863 our troubles only took a different form. 132 years after emancipation we still struggle against unbelievable conditions. I spoke briefly to many of these conditions in my first book, *Awaken: Creating a Blueprint for Enlightenment, Organization & Freedom*, so I won't repeat the list of human rights abuses and atrocities here.

However, there are some aspects of our existence in America and throughout the Western hemisphere that still need to be addressed. First, we need a visual reminder of our sojourn in America that will force us to look reality in the face. On the pages that follow, we get an inkling of the thousands of Africans lynched in America and a glimpse at the horrible ugliness underlying our existence in the United States.

Photo Courtesy of the Library of Congress

Crowd of European Americans gather in Texas for the lynching, involving a chain noose and torture by slow burning, of an 18-year-old African
named Jesse Washington. (Jesse's naked body is in the center of the picture
under the tree.) Photo Courtesy of the Library of Congress

A close up of the badly burnt body of 18-year-old Jesse Washington, still hanging by the neck from the tree. Photo Courtesy of the Library of Congress

The crowd looks on as Jesse Washington's body smolders, while still hanging from the tree. Photo Courtesy of the Library of Congress

An African hangs from a tree handcuffed and still in his blood stained dress clothes. Photo Courtesy of the Library of Congress

European Americans vie for a place in the picture around the burnt remains of William Brown. Photo Courtesy of the Library of Congress

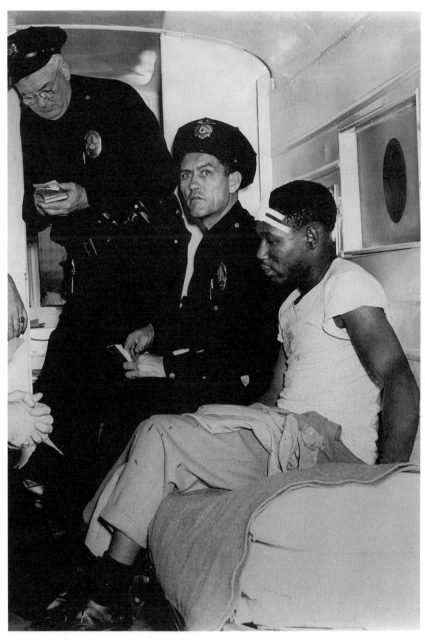

Lynchings take on the form of "brutality in blue."   Photo Courtesy of the Library of Congress

The sickness of lynching depicted in a portrait with a European American posing for the camera.   Photo Courtesy of the Library of Congress

We need to mourn these losses and this suffering so that we can progress clear headed and correct. It is dangerous to be naive, simple minded and in denial about the true reality of the African existence in the Western hemisphere. What is wrong with a people who pretend like they are welcome visitors capable of assimilating in a land where they were enslaved for hundreds of years and continue to receive constant reminders of the hostility they face? How deep in denial is that group of people who still strive after the valued possessions and mental attitudes of their oppressors, while refusing to engage in the necessary activities and long range planning necessary for true freedom of us all? Remember, if there are any among us who are not truly liberated because they are African, none of us are safe or secure. It could be you next! We've been tricked. The prognostication of Willie Lynch, in chapter three, that said that after our indoctrination during enslavement we would continue to be "self refueling and self generating for hundreds, maybe thousands of years," was too accurate. What a bitter taste this should leave in our mouths.

Just as we did with the Maafa, we need to take a look at resistance to the suffering that was represented in the images of the previous pages. One of the most powerful movements in the history of Africans in the Western hemisphere was that of Marcus Mosiah Garvey. Marcus Garvey aspired to African independence, self-sufficiency, and nation building. The movement philosophy and direction was the most uncompromisingly purposeful movement that we can examine.

Born in Jamaica in 1887, Garvey founded what was to be an international or global movement in 1914 at the age of 27. This organization was known as the Universal Negro Improvement Association (UNIA). In 1916, Garvey came to the United States where the UNIA was to find a major base of support.

Perhaps the most substantial aspect of this movement was in its philosophical direction of independence, cultural affirmation and institution building. Unlike other movements and organizations, such as the National Association for the Advancement of Colored People (NAACP) and the Civil Rights movement, Garvey was not looking to "fit in" to a European dominated society or to take a place next to the former slave master via assimilation and legal equity. Garvey believed in nation building and to that effect was able to accomplish a great deal.

Growing out of conscious resistance to mental, physical and cultural oppression and degradation, the UNIA established a newspaper called the *Negro World*, the Black Star Steamline Company, Black Cross Nurses, and even sent engineers and building materials to Africa for the purpose of beginning to build a nation. Also, at the first International Convention of the Negro Peoples of the World in 1920, held in Madison

Square Garden, Garvey and the UNIA attracted enough Africans to fill "the Garden," with residual crowds outside. Additionally, according to Dr. Clarke, "His organization was paramilitary with a respected officer corps." [8] The UNIA not only impacted the U.S. and the Caribbean, but opened branches in South Africa, among other places.

The vision was there for true freedom and equality. Unfortunately Garvey may not have sufficiently planned for and anticipated the obstacles that would be in his path. The beginning of the end came with his conviction, imprisonment and deportation based on a "legal lynching" for charges of mail fraud. Despite challenges to Garvey's business acumen and leadership skill, he has impacted Africans everywhere who knew him, knew of him, or have not been denied information on him through his omission from U.S. history textbooks.

Conscious resistance in a hostile environment of oppression cannot be viewed as radical. It is in fact a sign of normal behavior. The individual or group who does not resist when oppressed is abnormal. It is no different than an animal that is attacked and does not show the normal behavior of "fight or flight." The animal that freezes when attacked is abnormal, traumatized, or in some instances lulled into complacency and dazed confusion by a crafty predator. Again, CONSCIOUS RESISTANCE IN A HOSTILE ENVIRONMENT OF OPPRESSION CANNOT BE VIEWED AS RADICAL!

With this in mind, names like Marcus Garvey, Kwame Ture (Stokely Carmicheal), Assata Shakur, Sundiata Acoli, John Africa, H. Rap Brown, Elijah Muhammad, and many others, manifest the normal and valid behavior of resistance under the pressure of oppression. It's not particularly important whether you agree with their ideologies or not, the point is that they resisted.

To take it a step further, Elijah Muhammad's formation of the Nation of Islam (NOI) represented a profoundly appropriate transformation of religion. One's religion comes out of one's culture and particular circumstances, which is why European Christianity worships a European Jesus and has used religion, including portraying Jesus as a white man, to further their cultural and political agenda. What Elijah Muhammad did was take Islam and put it within the cultural context of the African existence in America. He shaped a religion designed to uplift and resist. In her book, *Yurugu*, Marimba Ani carries the concept of religion's cultural affinity, and especially European Christianity's cultural foundation as opposed to its proposed universality, to much deeper levels.

Beyond the complex religious components of Elijah Muhammad's movement, he too was a nation builder. The NOI developed schools, a newspaper, bakeries, grocery stores, health clinics, etc. The NOI strove toward self-sufficiency and self-determination. The teachings of Elijah Muhammad produced the brilliance of El Haaj Malik El Shabaaz (Malcolm X), as well as Minister Louis Farrakhan. They also produced the all important self defense arm called the Fruit of Islam (FOI). The strength and conviction of the NOI, and what has been seen as a   controversial ideology, did not develop in a void. Had there been no murdering, brutality, rape, misuse, and miseducation of the African   community, the NOI may not have come to exist. The NOI did not produce the environment that made them absolutely necessary in America.

****

From what has been examined in this chapter we should be, at the very least, on the road to a clear understanding of the links between our present conditions and the Maafa; and therefore the realization of the necessity for continued struggle, coupled with the global consciousness and connections of African people made in preceding chapters. In realizing these things, we will all be somewhere on the road to spiritual and emotional healing as a result of our dealing sanely with the past, consequently freeing our minds from the void of denial and ignorance of how we have come to be where we are in the world today.

CHAPTER 6

NATION BUILDING

You are not free; no matter how many seats you have in congress; no matter how many McDonald's and Coca Cola commercials people who look like you sing and dance in; no matter how many European's you're allowed to sit next to in restaurants; no matter how many entertainers and CEO's you have making millions. If your destiny is still controlled by someone else you are not free. In order to speak about true freedom for African people, we have to speak about being in control of our mental faculties, our destiny and direction as a people. In order to do that we must speak about controlling our educational, economic, social and cultural institutions: nation building. In this work nation building doesn't mean you *have* to go anywhere or section off a territory in the United States for Africans, although a sovereign nation will be discussed in Chapter 13. It means we must control where and what we are.

To build these institutions and be self-determined as a people requires unity. Hopefully, everything preceding this chapter of the book has affirmed for some and prepared others for the necessity of unity, global identification with all African people and action. We already have the guidance, knowledge and planning necessary to put us on the path. Chancellor Williams outlined a master plan in *The Destruction of Black Civilization*, which I referred to in *Awaken*. Williams also spoke to nation building for Africa in *The Rebirth of African Civilization*, which contained useful information for Africans everywhere. The planning of Chancellor Williams gives us a good place to begin in terms of looking at the capabilities for self-determination and nation building. Two areas to begin with are mass organization and the development of African Universities.

The idea of an African University is put forth in Williams' *The Rebirth of African Civilization*. While his work speaks specifically about meeting the needs of Africans on the continent, his ideas are certainly applicable to our global unity. In terms of a pedagogical approach and ideology, Williams offers some points that we can use and expound upon.

1. That the critical state of the world is directly due to the failure to make the primary object of all education and training the improvement of man himself -- his character, spiritual and moral potential, and his cooperative spirit for goodwill and fellowship, first with his immediate relations and then extending the attitude to the rest of the human family.

2. That much of all science and research on the university level should be directed expressly to this end.

3. That the sources of beneficial knowledge are almost indefinite and that, accordingly, no single discipline, classical or otherwise, can properly preempt the field of higher learning while, on the other hand, it is equally foolhardy to substitute training for a job or a profession for liberal education.

4. That there need be no conflict at all, once it is recognized that a democracy should offer equality of opportunity to all of its people to develop to the fullest extent of their varying capabilities, to receive a liberal education if they are intellectually able and desire it, and that this liberal education should be at once the foundation and prerequisite for higher occupations and professions and, most important, the system through which the development of better human beings, begun in the homes and elementary schools, is programmed and therefore consciously furthered.

5. That the emphasis must be deliberately shifted from rampant individualism with its competitive ideology of "every man for himself and the devil take the hindmost" to cooperation or mutual aid which, though played down, is as much a part of human nature as the aggressive tendencies we glorify.

6. That materialism and its offspring, competitive individualism, have served to check man's spiritual-moral advance, keeps him close to the lower animal world, and they have tended to limit his outlook to their level. This is unnecessary because all the extraordinary achievements of science and technology could be more fully appreciated and enjoyed if man himself were improved; and, finally

7. That both happiness of the human family and the probability of its continued existence on this planet, may rest entirely upon such improvement. It is difficult to see how nations of the world can continue to stagger along their present course, as though drawn along irresistibly by some siren's song, except to destruction. [1]

Williams sets forth clear thinking on the purpose and necessary direction of university education. From Williams' first point, the philosophy of our African Universities would be developed in our interests as African people first, but because of the spirituality and equity that we should bring into such an endeavor, our institutions would benefit all of humanity as well. These institutions would provide a learning atmosphere that nurtures African people and produces high scholarship, leadership, and vision, but this necessitates no conflict with the ability of these universities to service all people. The key aspect is that we will control these institutions and dictate their pedagogy and curriculum content in a manner that the West has failed to do with their institutions. If African people the world over can attend European institutions that are narrow, arrogant, and detrimental towards us, why can't Europeans and others attend our universities which will approach education in a much different, more human and all encompassing way? We have much to teach the world as a result of the wisdom that has been forged in the fire of struggle. (This applies not only to universities, but some of the other educational institutions that will be discussed later.)

However, the upliftment of Africans is our primary concern. First and foremost, this is because we are African people and we must take care of ourselves because no one else will. Secondly, if an Emergency Medical Technician (EMT) arrives at the scene of an accident and some people only have minor bruises while others have multiple lacerations, head trauma and have gone into cardiac arrest, the EMT will attend to those who need the most care first. Likewise our universities will have been developed to attend to us first. Europeans, Asians, Native Americans, Pacific Islanders and others are welcome to learn with us, but if they have different ideas about education, as European institutions have historically shown, then they can go back to their own institutions. Our African universities will not be co-opted or compromised and we will not span the globe begging for the participation of other cultural groups. We encourage it, but our conditions as a people around the world don't allow us the time to be *overly* concerned about others at present.

The other points Williams lists speak for themselves and I would only comment further on point seven. Seeing the destructive path that many in today's world are taking, namely Europeans being destructive not only to others but to themselves, we should not desire to go down with that which is going down. Neither should conscientious people of any kind make such a decision. The decision should be to rise with that which is rising and true. What is rising is the kind of self-determined, humane, truthful thought that Williams shares with us.

Being the meticulous planner and visionary that he was, Williams did not leave us with these general points of reflection. He went on to describe his vision or master plan which included the structure of the university. The many divisions and schools within the university are numerous and include the Division of Community Service, Board of Standards, Examinations and Degrees, Interdepartmental Coordinating Council, University Press, and Division of Research and Advanced Studies. There are also schools, institutes and colleges within the university which meet various academic needs such as professional training and specialization in different fields. All of this is laid out, with specific components of administration and content, by Williams.

As far as Williams' recommendations for mass organization, this too was extensively covered in *The Destruction of Black Civilization* and I referred to his ideas in my previous work *Awaken*. Therefore, I will simply leave you with the words of Chancellor Williams on this subject.

> It has been previously stated in substance that although African people may continue their present course of weakness on into the future with thousands of ununified organizations, powerless and, therefore forever dependent like half-men and half-women unable to use their own brains, although this tragic situation may continue into an uncertain future, we say it can never be said again that such a hopeless situation persists because no member of the race or any group has ever studied the principle problems and the obstacles to their solutions based on history, and then offered an overall plan as one of the possible lines of march out of the morass...
>
> In this section are the specifics of *a MASTER PLAN*. It is to be the functioning framework of a unifying Race Organization of a kind never presented to the black race before. [2]

It is from that point that Williams begins his enlightenment, wisdom that should be at least *considered* by all of us.

Like the planning and vision of Williams, we have many other models to follow in terms of our direction towards institution building in other areas. Haki Madhubuti gives examples of institution building in his life's accomplishments (i.e. Third World Press and New Concept Development Center) and in works such as *From Plan to Planet* and *Claiming Earth*. Brother Madhubuti has done wondrous things not only with his writing, but in his establishing of a publishing company like Third World Press, which has ensured that the voices of sane African people are heard abundantly.

We are in need of more institutions like Third World Press, Africa World Press, A & B Books, and others, to get our information and our story out. We need many more of these types of institutions. The New Concept Development Center, an elementary educational institution developed by Madhubuti, also gives us the opportunity to look at the aspect of education, without which universities are useless: elementary and secondary schools.

The independent school movement is growing stronger in America. Many African-centered independent schools and other alternative institutions are being developed to meet the needs of African children. In *Too Much Schooling, Too Little Education*, edited by Mwalimu Shujaa, some important questions are asked by Joyce Elaine King and Thomasine Lightfoote Wilson.

> Dare we search for a liberated pedagogy? What can be the impact of African liberation pedagogy in this political climate, especially when Black children are being held "hostage" in systems not designed to free them? How can these Black children function as themselves when African knowledge and culture are disrespected and people of African ancestry everywhere are under siege? [3]

Clearly, if we are serious about ourselves and our liberation we must come full circle in our belief in self determination and the need to take control of the maximization of our children's special potential. We are irresponsible if we complain about the conditions we face in America, as well as the overt and concealed hostility, yet we continue to give our children as a blind sacrifice (sending them to school) to the society we complain about.

Fortunately, this is changing. As mentioned above, the independent school movement is gaining momentum. This momentum is coming from quarters such as individuals who decide to develop schools, and also larger efforts of organization, such as the Institute for Independent Education in Washington D.C. Under the direction of Joan Davis Ratterray, the Institute for Independent Education conducts research, develops curriculum materials, publishes an information newsletter, forges links between institutions around the country and generally is serving as a vehicle for the perpetuation and constant evolution of the independent school movement to save African children. Useful publications from this same institute, such as *Start Your Own School: Ten Founders and Administrators Tell How*, serve to provide the information and framework for the continued development of these institutions.

The masses of African people have to move beyond rhetoric and endless complaining in this area of education. Essentially, all the protest and activism in the world is useless in the long run if our children are being educated in a way that is not conducive to continued struggle and self-determination. We'll find ourselves making short term gains, only to be thrown into the cycle of regression as future adults are lost to assimilation and complacency, and we spend inordinate amounts of time re-educating those who have maintained some spirit of resistance. This is much the situation now, as we have seen several cycles of resistance come and go with no substantive long term benefits in terms of African psychological, cultural, educational, and economic independence of the masses. There was a time back in the late 1700's when people like Richard Allen, the founder of the African Methodist Episcopal Church, were thinking consciously about self-determination. The fact that this early beginning wasn't generated into massive nation building can be partially attributed to the lack of communication and education necessitated by the Maafa, as well as our matriculation in European controlled settings, when available. The European educational hegemony played a large role in changing the sentiment of identification with Africa by the masses, seen in the name of Richard Allen's church, to a distancing from Africa in terms of our identity and cultural heritage. Consequently, we went through times much later when we regressed to being called Negroes, coloreds, and blacks; terms which we accepted and none of which grounded us in a way conducive to global struggle and knowledge of self. Amazingly, we came full circle to find ourselves grappling with whether to be called Afro Americans or African Americans, some two hundred years later.

This is just a brief anecdote to show how we spin our wheels when we don't seek self-determination and institutions in all areas of life. Specific emphasis is put on education because it can serve as an undergirding for all other activity. A properly educated individual might easily see the need to build economic institutions and be equipped to do so. A person properly attuned to the knowledge of themselves and their existence in America will take unity for granted and engage in action, viewing it as necessary and a given. That person will also willfully call themselves African, seeing the beauty, pride, cultural grounding, historical understanding and identification that goes along with this description.

These types of attitudes that may result from proper education are powerful and empowering. Of course this proper education must be in conjunction with the influence of other institutions, but it allows us to avoid the time consuming task of re-educating and convincing before we even get to planning and building for a future. In our present state as a people we often end up a lot of the time trying to convince our less conscious brothers and sisters that their education is insufficient and their existence in America is not peaches and cream. We try to convince them that there is in fact a reason for them to know more about themselves and their own history than they know about Europe and her history. We spend far too much time trying to undo the unhealthy and false assimilationist socialization that many of our brothers and sisters acquire through the educational system.

We must control and maintain elementary, secondary and university level institutions. Our circumstances dictate it and our future depends on it. We do not want to see the next generation thirty years from now, asking the same questions and dealing with the same hostile conditions, as they begin another cycle of resistance because we failed to build and create.

As we speak about the building of institutions and nation building in general, we must continue to be mindful that we need to forever be thinking in terms of African people worldwide. Thinking in this way and acknowledging our link with Africa, we cannot overlook its importance here. Of utmost importance to us is the progress of Africa towards true independence; which means economic control of their resources (currently controlled by Europe); political control and shedding of colonial corruptive influences, mentalities, and supported conflict; the dismantling of colonial educational structures that have always existed for the degradation and dependence of Africans; and the re-legitimizing of African culture, including language, art, history and dynamic traditional practices (dynamic in that they change to recognize changing times and needs).

This is of such major importance to us for several reasons. First of all, Africa is a place of grounding and return for African people around the world. It is the only place that we can look to and call home with any sense of comfort, welcome, ancestral tradition and warmth. Secondly, what many of us don't realize is that, in large part, as Africa goes we all go. Lack of political consciousness and power in Africa ensures our weakness in America, while African strength has traditionally strengthened us in America, the Caribbean and elsewhere. One only has to look to the late fifties and the sixties during the African independence wave and see the impact that it had on Africans everywhere in terms of the political awareness, action, and consciousness. Leaders such as Malcolm X (El Haaj Malik El Shabaaz) and Kwame Ture (Stokely Carmicheal) spoke of the victorious struggles of Africans fighting colonialism. Kwame Ture currently lives in Africa. The changing tide of independence on the continent also influenced the dawning of African clothing and the adoption of African names here in America.

On the other hand, the more that our home is defiled and disrespected, the more difficult it will be for us Africans in the Western hemisphere who continue to struggle, as we look to the glory of our Mother Continent for cultural and aesthetic sustenance. Finally, as a place of return and homeland, African needs to be a place where many of us can go back to, whether it is to live, to do business, to vacation, to work with our brothers and sisters, or to retreat if our existence becomes any more threatened than it already is in the Western hemisphere.

With Africa in mind, the late Chiekh Anta Diop, as one of our greatest minds, gave us much to consider. Not only did Diop do great work on restructuring African history, but he wrote about an African future along the lines of our focus on nation building. In his book, *Black Africa: The Economic and Cultural Basis for a Federated State*, Diop offered a tremendous wealth of information for us to examine.

The major focus of Diop's work in *Black Africa*, outside of the general establishment of an African Federated State, is with regard to his extremely sophisticated analysis of the utilization of resources in Africa and the development of energy sources. His trademark scientific thoroughness is epitomized regarding hydraulic, solar, atomic, thermonuclear, tidal, sea thermal, volcanic thermal and geothermal energies. Meticulous descriptions of these energy types are accompanied by their potential use in a Federated State. Further attention is paid to the resources and potential for industrialization in key regions of Africa.

In reading anything that Chiekh Anta Diop produced, it is easily recognizable that he was a scholar and scientist of awesome proportions. Diop was a historian and linguist of the highest degree. He was also a physicist who worked and studied in Paris at a major nuclear research facility. He went on to found his own radiocarbon laboratory in Dakar, Senegal. His amazing abilities are well described in a book edited by Ivan Van Sertima, another of our great thinkers, called *Great African Thinkers: Chiekh Anta Diop*. Van Sertima revealed that "At a time when only a handful of people in the world understood Einstien's relativity theory, Diop translated a major portion of it into Wolof, the language of his people." [4]

This reflects not only his scientific brilliance, but his consciousness as a fighter for African liberation. Diop also

> founded the *Block of the Masses of Senegal*, a militant political party in 1960. The party was banned and he was arrested and imprisoned. He founded a second political party in 1964, the *Senegalese National Front*. This was declared illegal and he was again arrested. He founded a third political party, the *National Democratic Rally*, in 1976. [5]

This conscious resistance and political/cultural consciousness also came through in Diop's book, *Black Africa*, as he not only equipped readers with detailed resource and energy information, but enumerated various steps necessary for the unity of African people. One of the necessary steps included in his analysis was "to restore consciousness of our historic unity," [6] which he did in his many writings, including *Civilization or Barbarism*, *The Cultural Unity of Africa*, and *African Origins of Civilization: Myth or Reality?*. Other steps articulated by Diop include working out "an effective form of representation for the female sector of the nation," and the move

> to work for linguistic unification on a territorial and continental scale, with a single African cultural and governmental language superseding all others; the European languages, then, whichever they may be, would remain in use or be relegated to the status of foreign languages taught in secondary schools [7]

Rarely does a man with the scientific ability and cultural consciousness of a Chiekh Anta Diop arise. His insights regarding the future of African unity are certainly still a viable goal and direction.

Dr. John Henrik Clarke, another of are revered minds, has given us *Notes for an African World Revolution*. As our elder statesmen, Dr. Clarke gives a historical account of revolutionary leaders and movements, as well as his view of where we are and how we need to develop as a people.

> We have seen many roads leading in many directions, and we read the signboards wrong. We went down roads that did not lead us home. We have to go back to the fork in the road and read those signboards again. We have to find the signboard that reads: Unity, African World Federation, Pan-Africanism, African Solidarity. When we see that on the board (the unification of all African people throughout the world, the self-interest of African people first, black and black unity, meaning more than black and white unity)... [8]

****

What will we do with this knowledge? First of all, we will do nothing if we don't study enough to grasp it. Secondly, we must move as a people in key areas.

1) African people are not monolithic and comprise many cultures, ideologies and philosophies. However, as a people we must be clear on certain points of consensus. As we realize that we have common obstacles to overcome in our worldwide struggle from the low depths of oppression, we must carry common value orientations in key areas, by which all of our action will be guided.

    * African people must decide that we will refuse to mistreat women in the way that they are being mistreated, undervalued, and devalued around the world, including the United States. Regardless of Western values, religious sexism, or outdated traditional beliefs, we as a people must make the decision to allow women to guide us to higher levels of humanity in every human endeavor. We must cease the abuse and the rape of women and abandon the mindset that allows it to enter our consciousness.

    * Material wealth must only be subordinate to strong families, self knowledge, sound relationships, the principles of Maat and the Nguzo Saba. The Nguzo Saba, developed by Maulana Karenga, might be recognized by some as the principles of Kwaanza. Nguzo Saba is a Swahili term which means "seven principles." These principles are useful for our liberation and unity and are as follows:

> Umoja (Oo-mo-jah), **Unity** - to strive for and maintain unity in family, community, nation and race.
> Kujichagulia (Koo-je-cha-gu-lia), **Self-determination** - to define ourselves, name ourselves, create for ourselves and speak for ourselves instead of being defined, named, created for and spoken for by others.
> Ujima (Oo-je-mah), **Collective Work and Responsibility** - to build and maintain our community together and make our sister's and brother's problems our problems and to solve them together.
> Ujaama (Oo-ja-maa), **Cooperative Economics** - to build and maintain our own stores, shops and other businesses and to profit from them together.
> Nia (Ne-ah), **Purpose** - to make our collective vocation the building and developing of our community in order to restore our people to their traditional greatness.
> Kuumba (Ku-um-ba), **Creativity** - to do always as much as we can in the way that we can in order to leave our community more beautiful and beneficial than we inherited it.
> Imani (E-m-ne), **Faith** - to believe with all our heart in our people, our parents, our teachers, our leaders, and the righteousness and victory of our struggle.

    The principles of Maat are also very useful for our upliftment, especially spiritually. These are discussed in greater detail in Chapter 14 entitled "The Ancient African Model."

 * We must educate, at the very least, 70% of our children. This is to mean that we must control the content, values and administration of their education. Our children must be viewed as our valued and cherished promise for a new tomorrow. From previous discussion it should be apparent why it is important for us to maximally develop our children instead of entrusting them to others.

 * We must defend ourselves physically and mentally. An organized, disciplined, well trained, warrior contingent will be necessary for our physical protection. The time has passed for our churches being bombed and organizations and people attacked, as we only watch and cry out.

A responsive, proactive and consciously directed system of print and electronic media must be our mental defense against the onslaught of negative, divisive images and propaganda that we are constantly and intentionally bombarded by.

 * We must build our own national and international economic institutions.

The means by which various people approach these points of consensus will necessarily vary.

2) A matter of critical importance is our long term direction. We as a people, whether through a mass organization representative of the views of the masses or some other means, must have specific and clearly defined long term objectives. Such objectives are necessary and must be kept in the front of people's consciousness to ensure the direction, clarity of purpose and continuous, uncompromising nature of our struggle.

A retrospective example from the Civil Rights movement can be used for clarity. If a clear objective, understood and articulated by the masses, would have been economic, social and cultural equality defined as African people being in control of our own destiny and self-determined in these areas as a people, the result of this struggle may have been different. Sitting in restaurants, attending universities and working in corporations run by Europeans may not have been enough to contribute to the pacifying of many former "activists," the dissipation of a mass movement and the perceived absence of a struggle that persists among far too many Africans today. With clear and well defined objectives the struggle continues until these objectives are met, regardless of what small and illusory concessions are made on the road to the end objectives. It must be conceded that hindsight is 20/20. However, as judgemental as it may sound, this is how we learn from our mistakes.

There must be no confusion between tactics and objectives/strategy. A tactic is defined as "An expedient for achieving a goal: a maneuver." [9] The fact that a tactic is an "expedient" and the strategy is the goal itself and means of achieving it, allows a distinction to be made. What has often happened to us is we have been tricked into believing that our tactics are our strategy. In other words, in the heat of battle we believed that the tactics of sit-ins and integration legislation were our strategy, when actually these were tactics that were part of the strategy to secure freedom, justice and equality.

At no time in America have we been truly free, received justice or equality, so where is the struggle now? Where is that sustained mass movement? (If you do believe that we have attained true freedom or equality, you haven't done enough studying, haven't looked closely at the definition of freedom, justice and equality, and certainly haven't looked at the reality of life in America for most of our African brothers and sisters.)

3) There must be many who participate in the formulation of our objectives and strategy. However, some thought provoking suggestions follow.

* We insist that Africa be a continent made up of truly independent nations that can no longer be referred to as "Third World" and wield true power on the world stage, operating as a block of countries with common interests. This would include having control over the richness of their land and the utility of its numerous people.

* Africans throughout the diaspora should look to the Mother Continent of Africa for support and a political and cultural base of power, and vice versa. A similar situation exists, and grows stronger, with Israel and diasporan Jews.

* Formation of African Universities, elementary and secondary systems, etc., to educate at least 70% of African children. (It is estimated 70% because [a] there will be those who hold on to assimilationist viewpoints and reject African run institutions and [b] we need *some* of our stronger brothers and sisters to report back to us on what is taking place in the European institutions and community. They of course would have enough of a support structure to make sure they don't become victims of these institutions they are monitering.)

* Formation of World African Banks and other economic institutions. There is sufficient capital in the African community of the United States alone to invest in the establishment of banks for the maintenance of this tremendous cash reserve. (If Africans in America were considered a nation, we would rank amongst the top ten countries in the world based on monetary wealth.)

* There must be conscious, unified mass communication links between Africans in Africa, the Caribbean, North, South and Central America, and wherever else they exist. There must be shared educational exchange between African Universities; shared economic and resource exchange (trading); and shared cultural and social validating activities and institutions.

* The linking of African people globally must include specific long term planning. For instance, substantial numbers of Africans in America must be assigned and must volunteer to learn Portuguese for the express purpose of linking with the masses of Africans in Brazil, where Portuguese is a dominant language. Still larger numbers of Africans in America, the Caribbean and Brazil (and all of South America) must be schooled in African languages such as Wolof, Hausa, Yoruba, Kiswahili, Nubian, Igbo, Kikongo, Zulu, Xhosa, etc., for the express purpose of forming vital and mutually meaningful links with our African brothers and sisters on the continent.

The list could go on and on. The tactics and operating principles are another matter for discussion, study, long term planning and consensus.

4) Time has taught critical observers of history that when African people move towards self-determining and mass organizational endeavors, we are moved against with sometimes barbaric force. This can be seen in the FBI's undermining of Civil Rights organizations and personalities through programs like COINTELPRO. It can be seen in the exile of Assata Shakur and the political imprisonment of Geronimo Pratt. It can be seen in worldwide government destabilization, especially of "third world" governments, in the form of Western support for ruthless dictators, drug cartels, military coups, etc.

Sometimes the motivator is racism. Sometimes the motivator is world management or "the new world order," which depends on "manageable democracies" (i.e. elite rich control over the mindless masses) and necessitates destabilized, dependent populations capable of being manipulated and exploited. These manageable democracies can then be exploited and manipulated by coalitions of international, rich and elite men such as the Trilateral Commission and member multinational corporations. The exploitation and manipulation takes place not only in Africa and other "third world" countries, but also right in America where the rich get richer, the poor get poorer, and international trade barriers fall to GATT (General Agreement on Tariffs and Trade) and NAFTA (North American Free Trade Agreement) type agreements which ensure the continuation of the trend.

It should be noted here that these tenuous relations of the African community to those "new world order" advocates and Trilateralists is further complicated in the area of education. Previous discussion of education has not included the fact that such people as Trilateral "Commissioners urge a reexamination of higher education--hoping to make less room for opposition and alienation to develop." [10] Since opposition to the status quo is essential in our struggle, these types of Trilateralist educational policies are threatened by the development of African Universities, secondary and elementary schools. In developing our own institutions we seek liberation through opposition, resistance, enlightenment and high level scholarly achievement. Again, this is opposed by certain forces in the Western hemisphere, as is further illustrated by the following remarks describing Trilateral Commission policy.

> Like democracy, education must be limited--serving the needs of the ruling class... Commissioners recommend that more teenagers be steered away from college toward vocational training and that an attempt be made to lower the career expectations of "surplus" people with college degrees. In both cases these measures are aimed first and foremost, not at the traditionally educated white male elite, but at minorities and women who fill the lower levels of the work force. [11]

Though these relationships are complex and cannot be fully explained in a couple of paragraphs, the simple message is that our unity and progress will engender hatred and forceful aggression from many quarters. We must be prepared to operate as cleverly as possible, but also be able to defend ourselves by means of organized armed forces. This again is long term planning. Like most of what we need to do, the specifics will not and cannot be written in any book. They simply must be done.

The other area of defense is having a strong enough foothold of independently African owned radio stations, television stations, newspapers, magazines, movie theaters, movie studios, publishing companies, book stores, etc., to disseminate positive information that counteracts the barrage of negative imagery of African people in American print and electronic media. The necessity of this should be evident from the attacks on African people in magazines such as Time and Newsweek, in books which espouse racist ideology, derogatory television and movie production, and biased newscasts to name a few. (Though there are specific instances to better illustrate this point, none are given [a] because they are only variations on old themes, many of which were dealt with in my previous book, *Awaken*, and [b)] negative press and images do not warrant any more attention by appearing here.)

Aside from the everyday negative images and media attacks on our character, we can refer back to the concept of governable democracy, alluded to earlier.

> How do the trilateralists propose to make democracy more governable? In the age where the media is considered the most effective means of reaching the "hearts and minds" of the population, steps must be taken to strengthen the symbiosis between media and government. [12]

In other words, the media, which in large part is owned by the rich elite interests, becomes a tool of controlled information and propaganda.

****

After having investigated some areas in which we must operate as a people, we need to look at some ways in which individuals can begin to make an impact in our struggle today, right now.

1) Self Knowledge: Each of us should utilize what time we have to study and learn about ourselves, in terms of our glorious cultural history, how we have come to be where we are in the world today and what our present conditions are as individuals within a world African community. This could mean reading books, participating in study groups or simply engaging in critical debate and discussion with conscious individuals.

2) Action: Each of us should ask ourselves each day "What have I done today to help improve life for myself, my family, and my people?" If the answer is "nothing," we need to change something in our next day's activities. This could mean things as simple as volunteering to mentor students at local schools, supporting positive organizations that might do the work you don't have the time for, joining organizations to contribute to the liberation of African people, teaching your own children about themselves and loving them, reading some portion of a book that furthers your consciousness, etc. It could also mean things that are more complex such as planning for institution building. For example, concrete endeavors such as independent schools, grocery stores, banks, credit unions, cultural organizations and defense organizations take specific planning and foot-work.

No matter how big or small each person's daily action may be, we must all contribute something everyday to our struggle.

3) Attitude: Often an attitude change comes with study, self knowledge and action. All of our attitudes must be forever moving towards a love for people, places and things that are African. We cannot be afraid to say "brother" or "sister" to one another and perpetuate unity on a personal level. We must love ourselves and the fullness of our lips, width of our noses and whatever hues of black, yellow, red and brown we happen to wear. We must also always be thinking of ways in which we might uplift or teach others as we ascend to greater accomplishments of knowledge, wealth, unity and prosperity.

4) Money: While there is nothing inherently wrong with material possessions, we must be careful in our acquisition of material things. Money and material things cannot be our prime objective in life. I have long preferred Haki Madhubuti's definition of success, which is "the maximization of one's natural gifts and talents for a fruitful and mean-ingful life for one's self, family and people." [13]

Along with this mental conception of money, we need to become conscious of practical financial money saving techniques. We need to save money and invest what we save in long term independence or self determining institutions.

Simple things such as paying off existing debt on credit cards and ceasing to use them are possible ways of making a person less dependent on a job (maintaining status quo at work so that the Visa, Master Card and Discover bills are not in jeopardy of becoming overdue if the job is threatened). Less dependence makes one more independent and capable of having more resources available for financial security, if not independence in the form of entrepreneurship and institution building.

Of course, money becomes more complex than this, but the more one knows concerning money and its management, the easier life becomes in this world. A life not spent worrying solely about survival can be channeled towards more productive activities and mental energies in our struggle.

5) Child preparation: This has been listed as a separate point because what is meant by child preparation here is that we must prepare our children for the hostile, unfriendly, racist society they will all have to encounter at some point or another. Many African people fail to spend time with their children preparing them for the nature of oppression and its obstacles. Consequently our children go into a mean society unprepared and are victimized, miseducated, confused, emotionally hurt, psychologically damaged and generally tossed to the wolves. Some make it just fine, while many others don't. The miseducated, assimilation minded, self-hating, European valued African child is just as much a casualty as the criminal minded, self-hating child in the inner city. That is why this point deserved special attention.

Part of preparing a child is honestly and constructively confronting the many issues that he or she will face. An example of a proactive approach is making sure that your child has toys, dolls and pictures in his or her own image. We cannot underestimate the psychological impact of these early images. It is the beginning of self-hatred when the child is surrounded with toys, dolls and pictures that *only* portray European children and adults engaging in fun, as well as serious activities. It is the beginning of self-hatred when that same child prefers European images to images that look like him or her. There have been studies that have shown African children rejecting dolls that look like them in favor of European dolls. Not only is this a rejection of the doll, but it is a rejection of self-image with a preference for the image of someone else.

So, as small a thing as it may seem to surround a child with self-affirming images, it is a critical step in preparing a child for the psychological beating he or she will take from the world we live in. As the child grows older and begins to read, this same principle should be applied to reading materials. There should be plenty of materials depicting and describing African children and adults laughing, smiling, playing, working, serious minded, loving and all of the other areas of life. There should be images of African doctors, lawyers, activists, participants in the struggle, mothers, fathers, sanitation workers, gardeners, teachers and every other occupation and responsibility that contributes to life and living.

Another example of child preparation is the necessary task of sitting a child down as soon as he or she is able to understand and telling that child very bluntly about racism, white supremacy, the Maafa and the current existence of African people in America. It is only fair and sane to prepare children for what they will face and give them insight into why the world is the way it is. By doing this the child is not only prepared for what he or she will most likely experience, but the child also has a headstart on succeeding regardless of what he or she will face. A child prepared in this way will be able to manuever successfully through this world not only for himself or herself, but also for African people.

It is imperative that we not leave our children out in the cold as far as the knowledge of themselves and the reality of the world they live in. It is OUR job to protect them for they are only children.

★★★★

With all of this information, it should not be difficult to formulate a vision of what we could accomplish. Envision, if you will, the future.

The majority of Africa has united in the form of a Federation of African States which Diop wrote of, or a United States of Africa which Tom Mboya of Kenya envisioned. Consequently, Europe has lost economic, political and educational control over the Federated States of Africa. There only remains some semblance of Arab control in North Africa which is falling rapidly as the Federated States of Africa have begun to provide resources, education and military might to the oppressed Nubian Africans in Egypt, as well as the Africans in the Sudan.

With this Federated States of Africa has come true independence from Europe and the realization of interdependence on behalf of Africans continent wide. Consequently, there is no longer talk about population problems on the African continent, because Africa's resources stay in Africa, from the raw material stage to the manufactured product stage, to meet the needs of Africans before resources leave the country for the benefit of trade. Also, with the recapturing of land and life sustaining agriculture, European controlled cash crops no longer take food out of the mouths of the hungry.

This economic and political revolution was interdependent on and inseparable from the educational revolution that occurred with the development of African Universities designed to meet the intellectual, social, technological and cultural needs of Africans. The development of these institutions, and their "feeder" elementary and secondary schools, played a significant role in economic and political independence, but at the same time was possible because of it. Native African languages have become the languages of education and the significant works of Europe have been translated from German, French and English into Wolof, Kikongo, Igbo, Kikuyu, etc. Even with this, the Federated States of Africa found it necessary to employ the use of a common language for the facilitation of Federation-wide activities. Swahili was the language adopted and is now spoken throughout the continent when different regions and cultural groups come together to do business, conduct intellectual exchange or share in cultural richness.

The adoption of Swahili by the Federation was also important as it relates to the events that have transpired in the African Diaspora. In North America, the boom of the independent school movement and the mass political and economic organizations ushered in a new age of consciousness. Swahili was easily adopted and utilized by the Africans in America during their organizational efforts and fascilitated a large part of the communication between Africans in America and those on the continent.

What took place in North America cannot be viewed in isolation or solely with regard to the developments on the African continent. It was in fact hemispheric unity, of the over 35 million Africans in North America with over 65 million Africans in Brazil, and many more millions in the Caribbean and the rest of South and Central America, which allowed events to progress as they have.

One of the initial steps was a massive, organized campaign for Africans in America to learn Portuguese and the political and cultural history of Brazil, in order to form task forces and think tanks capable of making viable connections with the masses of Africans in Brazil. African Brazilians were adopting Swahili as well, which was to replace already existing communications in English and those developing in Portuguese. All the while, the already strong connections between Africans in America and Africans in the Caribbean were being nurtured and empowered.

As in Africa, the development of African Universities, and their feeder schools, on a massive scale did much to contribute to the level of consciousness and unified world view necessary for global organization. Worsening conditions and exposed contradictions in America also catalyzed and accelerated unity on a mass scale throughout the hemisphere. The resultant activities and proper education led to the development of many African Diasporan Think Tanks, African Diasporan Political Lobbies, and African Diasporan Media Consortiums. The political consciousness of African people in America has also changed to one of independence to be respected and feared by the American political structure. The American political structure can no longer manipulate, but must please African people in America for survival.

On the international stage, the African political consciousness has progressed to the point where the Federated States of Africa have mass support and headquarter power bases in North America, Canada, Costa Rica, Brazil, Jamaica, Barbados, Cuba, Haiti and the Bahamas. There is also mass dual citizenship. Many Africans in America, for example, are citizens of both United States of America and the Federated States of Africa. These developments have erased the dependence of Africans in the Western hemisphere on their respective governments. As a consequence, Africans can truly call places like America their home away from home, knowing that their power and place of return, if necessary, is in the Federated States of Africa. They find comfort also in the fact that much of their suffering in what was a hostile environment has been alleviated and relations with other groups of people are more respectful and truly equitable.

The partnership and interdependence of Diasporan and Continental Africans also yielded the development of The World African Bank. This bank *effectively pooled the resources of African nations and people, serving as the final link to release former African nations from the grip of the World Bank and International Monetary Fund.*

These are just a few of the developments that have taken place, none of which occurred without difficulty. For example, the organization of the Federated States of Africa was met with subversion, infiltration and overt military aggression on the part of the world powers. There was bloodshed and conflict, which included the removal of African "sell outs" working for the Mossad and CIA against African unification. Fortunately the organization and sophistication of the overall African world community had reached a point where it was self perpetuating and could not be stopped by obstacles that had destroyed movements and progress years before. African military genius became reminiscent of Hannibal, Shaka and Queen Nzinga. The broad based unity of African people throughout the world had also already reached a level too far advanced to be easily undermined and powerful enough to influence world events, bringing tremendous pressure to bear in the backyards of the aggressive world powers. Huge portions of the world powers' militaries were negated because of the pullout of masses of Africans and other people of color. This was the mildest example of the type of pressure brought to bear in aggressive countries.

In America, where dual citizenship was initiated, attempts were made to pass legislation outlawing the dual citizenship provisions. By this time, however, the Federated States of Africa had sufficient control to bring multinational corporations to their knees by severing their ability to do any business at all with Africa, which led to pressure being put on the purse strings of American government and the abandonment of the legislation. Business ties were then restored, but under African conditions and interests, instead of the former conditions of exploitation.

Happily, though extremely confusing to Western analysts, the Federated States of Africa have not adopted the paradigm of exploitation, miseducation and imperial aggression held by the West. European, Asian and other students have matriculated in African Universities around the world and contributed to the upliftment and education of their own masses, as well as the ideological defense of the Federated States of Africa and their Diasporan population.

Some futurists predict a return of world equilibrium that has not existed since the Africans of ancient Kemet (Egypt) held their magnificent place at the head of civilization. The Africans in returning to their sources of ancestral knowledge and principles, along with their modern ingenious usurpation of injustice and oppression, have re-humanized the world.

Much of the success can be attributed to the beautiful African women who now hold prominent positions in every aspect of leadership, education, culture and economics. Some even attribute the positive and truly complete nature of the African world struggle to the women who began to figure visibly in leadership during the time when visionaries, writers, and activists alike moved to break the mental chains of mistreatment of women.

All of the great strides that have been made are equally impressive because they rest on a foundation built on justice, equality, enlightenment, and spirituality. Therefore, unlike the empires and powers of the modern West that were built on theft, oppression and murder, the Federated States of Africa and its children in the African Diaspora should rival the thousands of years of splendor that their African forbears enjoyed at the onset of civilization. It brings to mind the words of Marcus Mosiah Garvey as he said "Up, up you mighty race! You can accomplish what you will."

A Declaration

How long can you beat a man before he strikes back, oppressors
beware
How long can we cry and curse at home, but in public hold our
anger in a silent stare
What is coming? It must be coming, the day is not far
When the victim becomes the victor, no longer wishing on a star
There will be no freedom without bloodshed, for the rulers of the
world have a grip that's tight
Because soon survival is not enough, and the struggle becomes an
all out fight
The wrath of God has taken its time and not yet kindled against
the wicked makers of his-story
How long can babies die, mothers cry, people bleed, and the beast
feed, before the revolutionary assumes the glory
Not in one country, one city, one town or state
But around the world, African people, in unity before it's too late

Move on African people, move on. We have been kind and forgiving for too long. There is no longer any honor in turning the other
cheek or "getting along." The honor is in building and creating for our
children so that they don't have to turn the other cheek, they only have to
hold their heads high. The honor is in setting an example for the way
humanity operates by building our own institutions for self-determination
and simply failing to exploit *others*, not failing to defend *ourselves*. Move on
African people, move on.

Sick and tired of being sick and tired, I heard someone say. Many
of us are too young to be sick and tired, so tears are not enough to quell
our frustrations. Reciprocity must pay a visit on the world and we will
consider ourselves well rested. Move on African people, move on.

No sense in marching to the slaughter house, it must be different
this time. The beast will not lay down or roll over because we raise voices,
fists or weapons. In fact, the beast is ruthless enough to take the first born
children at the smell of trouble brewing amongst the masses. We have to

be wise, sure, strong, courageous, calculated and true. We must come like a thief in the night, a cancer that has defeated the body before the mind knows. Only this is no cancer, it is truth and justice. It is swift and "sharper than any two edged sword." The beast must blink once and find us around its throat, the jugular already cut. Move on African people, move on.

Can you just live in peace and try to improve yourself with a murderer, a beast, in your house? No! As much as you may hate blood and love life, you must clear your house of the danger the beast represents to you and your family. Strong words? Yes. They read as the Bible, everything is not as it seems, but it is there. Move on African people, move on.

PART III
CRITICAL AFTER-THINKING

CHAPTER 7

TEACHING THE MAAFA

As we look toward the many considerations that must be taken into account after the information that has been presented in this book, we return to the initial focus which is the Maafa or Great Suffering. Having presented all of this information on the Maafa and its implications as they affect African people even today, one practical matter of importance becomes the issue of teaching the Maafa. It is obviously a subject worthy of examination and understanding by every African child, as well as adult. It is a topic integral to knowledge of self. Further, the Maafa is so significant that it has and does impact the lives of everyone in the World in one way or another.

It is beyond doubt that in the Western hemisphere of this world all people, not just Africans, have been affected by the Maafa, in the following ways to list a few.

1) People who have come in contact with or been influenced culturally, and otherwise, by Africans who are in the Western hemisphere as a result of the Maafa.

2) People or groups of people who have been affected by the political, economic, military and cultural influence of America, a country whose existence is intricately linked to the Maafa.

3) People who have benefited directly or indirectly from the free labor and exploitation of Africans during and after the Maafa.

In the rest of the world the impact of the Maafa is also felt in:

1) The depopulation and subsequent colonization of the African continent by those who benefited from the Maafa.

2) The worldwide contact that various cultural groups have had with perpetrators of the Maafa and colonization, namely Germany, Italy, Portugal, Spain, England, America, etc. Japan, Korea, China, Vietnam, the Philippines, Pacific Islanders, New Zealanders and Australians have all dealt with these colonizers at one point or another and most have also had some interaction or contact with Africans. India is an example of an exploited land and people who fell under the greed and barbarity of the same British government who exploited Africa, and consequently Indians have had contact with Africans the world over. In African countries such as Azania (South Africa) and Uganda, Indians have lived in large populations. The Chinese had to deal with British immorality in the Opium War. Vietnam saw the aggression of the United States in the Vietnam War. The Phillipines have experienced U.S. and Spanish imperialism. Hawaii and other Pacific Islands have fallen prey to this same U.S. imperialism. Aboriginal Australians continue to see their world destroyed by European Australians who emigrated from England. The list is long.

With this presented, it is clear that no group of people in the world can escape the history of the Maafa. Therefore, it follows logically that the teaching of the Maafa in the shaping of today's world applies not only to Africans, but everyone. This is magnified by the technological advances that make the world a smaller and smaller place, where most of the world's cultural groups and nations have some interaction with the rest of humanity.

At this point, before considering pedagogy, it is important to deal briefly with a debate that arises and will arise whenever you talk about teaching the Maafa and other cultural content that is contrary to current "mainstream" curriculum. The debate we're speaking of is the debate that rages over "multiculturalism" and African-centered education. We will first deal briefly with multiculturalism, because there is much confusion, sometimes intentional, that surrounds the term and its substance. Part of what ensures confusion and ambiguity in the multicultural debate, notwithstanding racism and attempts to maintain the "status quo" socialization function of education, is the lack of precision implicit in the term multiculturalism or multicultural.

Many who have proposed multiculturalism have spoken of the importance of representing the perspectives and worldviews of various cultural groups in the educational process. This has rightly been suggested as a desired component of multiculturalism by prominent people such as Jawanza Kunjufu, Molefi Asante and James A. Banks. James A. Banks in particular, whose work frequently appears in educational journals, refers to this component of multicultural education as *transformation* of curriculum content as opposed to *infusion* of additional information into the existing curriculum.[1] In other words the perspectives of different cultural groups must be taken into account and transform the meaning and interpretation of material, rather than simply adding information to the existing content.

Where language precision enters the picture is in the fact that multiculturalism, or multicultural, by definition simply means that multiple cultures are *represented* and makes no specification as to whose *perspectives* these multiple cultures are viewed from. Consequently a textbook curriculum could technically be multicultural, because it deals to some degree with other cultures, and still be Eurocentric in its interpretation of information, allowing voices like Diane Ravitch and Aurthur Schlesinger to defend the current educational system claiming that it is already multicultural. These same "scholars" slander what they call "particularistic multiculturalism" or multiculturalism which deals particularly with African, Latin, Asian and other cultures.

As Madhubuti said, use language or be used by it. If we *use* language, my development of and utilization of the functional term, "multicentric" or "multicentricity," is for the express purpose of being more precise and clear in the goals of multiculturalism. Multicentric by definition means the representation of multiple cultures from multiple "centers" or perspectives. When one breaks the word down, "multi" means multiple cultures in this context, and "centric" means the center or frame of reference being used. Thus, implicit in the word multicentric is the representation of multiple worldviews or perspectives, a specification that is absent in the definition of multicultural and must be specifically articulated as a component of the concept.

A simple centric example would be in the handling, in history texts, of the interaction between Columbus and the Arawak people he encountered in the Caribbean. Not only would the European view of this interaction or "New World" encounter be given, but we would also gain the perspective of the Arawak who were witnessing the arrival, to their home, of people they were not familiar with and, as they found out, would destroy their lifestyles.

Another obvious example is the handling of the Maafa in curriculums. Currently many European centered texts:

a) deal inadequately in a quantitative way with the Maafa
b) refer to it as the Slave Trade, the inappropriateness of which has previously been discussed
c) give a European view speaking of the docility of the "slaves," the hopelessness of their condition and spend inordinate amounts of time speaking of and classifying the Maafa as commerce

These are just a few of the ways in which the lack of an African perspective can be seen, a situation remedied in the specificity of the term multicentric. Anything considered multicentric would have to take a perspective from an African point of view to satisfactorily deal with the Maafa; perhaps a view such as the one offered in this book could be used. This is the case because the Maafa happened to Africans. In like manner, when the suffering and annihilation of Native Americans is dealt with in a multicentric context, it must be from the Native American point of view.

Now, some qualifications must be made regarding this discussion of multicentricity. It is impossible for any one person or group of people to offer a multicentric approach totally absent of any of their own cultural interpretation. In other words, no one can separate themselves from their personal beliefs, work or pedagogical views.

Therefore if I, as an African person sanely grounded in who I am and my culture, produce a curriculum, it is of necessity and by definition African-centered in presentation and structure. At the same time, however, I may elect to take into account and present the perspectives of the various cultural groups I intend the curriculum to address. By taking these differing perspectives into account and using them in my curriculum, I am producing a multicentric curriculum.

Although this may sound confusing at first, it would be less confusing if these premises and definitions were understood and recognized prior to the cloud of emotional and distorted debate that currently rages. It would also render the debate that now rages more clear, precise and productive because of precise definitions.

So, what does it mean that a person or group always brings their own perspective even when utilizing a multicentric approach? Looking at African-centered pedagogy will allow us to gain some insight on this question. First of all, those who criticize Afrocentricity and even some proponents of it are confused or ignorant of the concept. In its purest articulated form, Molefi K. Asante is clear about the fact that Afrocentricity is inclusive and takes into account the perspectives of other cultures. It simply approaches knowledge construction and presentation from an African perspective, which is normal for African people.

Confused and ignorant critics of Afrocentricity, as a concept, often equate it with a sort of "reverse racism." Africans who misunderstand Afrocentricity often see it and use it as an exclusive study of Africa and her people. Both of these opinions are miscontrued. So, what of the move to institute Afrocentric education in school systems that are predominately African but still have students of other cultural groups? There are many inner city school systems, who are seeking to institute Afrocentric education. This seems to be a move on the part of such school systems to replace a distorted, detrimental, exclusive, often inherently oppressive Eurocentric education with an inclusive, multicentric, liberatory, more balanced African perspective. It is not replacing European intellectual hegemony with African hegemony. Current European pedagogy, in America on the whole, may present information on different cultures, but views all of humanity from the European perspective almost exclusively. An example is that the European murder of Native Americans in history is referred to as "conquest" or "victory" and Native American successful defensive counterattacks and victory are referred to as "massacres" and "savagery."

So, if one is going to use terms and labels for educational approaches, a general goal can be multicentricity regardless of what cultural worldview or centeredness is producing the education. Eurocentricity has failed (or suceeded depending on whose interests and ulterior motives we speak of) and Afrocentricity is not its equivalent, but a superior ideological philosophy at present.

With all of this said, teaching the Maafa can be clearly placed into the context of today's muddled educational mix. First, the human suffering and long term ill effects of the Maafa must be recognized. As examined in this book, this is possible without any serious excoriation of those by whom the most accountability must be taken for the suffering of the Maafa. This is not to say that excoriation, moral condemnation and accountability are not necessary, but sometimes in getting ourselves together we must focus on ourselves and necessary action, rather than diluting our concentration and attention with considerations of other people.

Secondly, the historical continuum of which the Maafa is a part must be admonished and used to complete the "big historical picture" which allows us to relate and identify with Africans everywhere. Thirdly, the African must see the truth of the resistance and lack of shame in being a child of the Maafa in order to use the experience for inspiration and continued struggle.

As a fourth point, the teaching of the Maafa also falls in line with the preparation of our children for success, as well as survival, in a hostile environment. It equips our children, as well as adults, with a large piece of the puzzle of how they fit in the world and what agenda their times dictate. It also provides models of success, perseverance, skilled oration, strong will, encyclopedic knowledge and all the tools and inspirations to nurture a hunger for knowledge.

Within the context of African-centered pedagogy, Agyei Akoto writes about some of the goals of African-centered education which apply to the teaching of the Maafa.

A potent transoceanic and transnational bond among Afrikans reflects the depth of the original cultural homogeneity among pre-colonial Afrikans as well as the gross and undifferentiated inhumanities of the holocaust of enslavement, colonial domination, and neocolonialism. Consequently, Afrikan-centered education within Afrikan-American communities or in Ghana, Zimbabwe, or Azania operates on the same principles and has the same goals. The essential goals are to achieve genuine self-sufficiency and self-determination. In each national context Afrikan-centered education seeks to develop the knowledge and skills needed to purge the process of education itself and the nation as a whole of the perverse effects of current, recent, and remote domination. Language, values, behaviors, images, systems, institutions, and relationships must all be thoroughly and critically re-examined. [2]

Finally, the teacher of this information must teach it from the view of reverence and relevance which it deserves, with a clear understanding of the culture of Africans before and after this tragedy. It is not to be seen as information or events incidental to American history or simply as African history, but as an inextricable part of world history and present realities. As such, it is important to every child and not a cross for the African child to bear.

The Maafa shouldn't be addressed in isolation from the rest of history. While special time may be devoted to intense study, the Maafa should be presented as one of the major events on the world historical continuum. This alone does a lot to place the onus of this disaster on all children to study it and understand it, instead of singling out the African student, which is often embarrassing and induces feelings of shame.

Of course the mindset, action and language of those who teach must also be correct, a consideration which leads us into the next chapter.

CHAPTER 8

LANGUAGE REVISITED

As we revisit the importance of language we should be mindful of all that his been said so far about it, as well as heeding the admonitions of Kwame Ture (Stokely Carmicheal) in his book *Black Power: The Politics of Liberation.*

> We shall have to struggle for the right to create our own terms through which to define ourselves and our relationship to the society, and to have these terms recognized. This is the first necessity of a free people, and the first right that any oppressor must suspend. [1]

Ture goes on to describe the control that "those who have the right to define" have over those they define. He shares that "This control includes the attempt by the oppressor to have *his* definitions, *his* historical descriptions, *accepted* by the oppressed." [2]

This is more than appropriate in our changing the way *we* define and the way *we* describe the Maafa. It manifests in our use of the term Maafa. It must manifest itself in our refusal to *accept* anything less than the tremendous significance we assign to the Maafa. It must manifest in our reference to those who suffered, as Africans or enslaved Africans, rather than "slaves." Yes they were enslaved and considered slaves, but our reference to them only as slaves strips their humanity and their unique human characteristics beyond their circumstance of enslavement. We must cease reference to the kidnapping and brutalization of our ancestors as "exportation," " importation" or "trade." We are also not "immigrants" to America as some widely used elementary and secondary social science textbooks refer to us. (Only those Africans from the continent, who have recently traveled to the United States for their education, business and other reasons, can be considered immigrants.) African people were enslaved and held captive in the most brutal manner. We did not chose to be in the Western hemisphere. This captivity and enslavement is not a description of immigration. Immigration means settling or moving to a place that is not one's native land. The definition does not account for capture or forced movement under enslavement. On the other hand, "exile" is a term that is very appropriate for African people in the Western hemisphere, since it does account for forced removal from one's native land. So we find ourselves currently in the position of exiles from Africa as a result of the Maafa.

The general picture of language as a tool should be understood at this point regarding our reference to the Maafa, but as we revisit the issue we need to look at language in other areas. For example, Native Americans were not "savages" that lived in "tribes" before Europe's destructive arrival, but native people who consisted of many different "nations." The use of "nation" as opposed to "tribe" deserves a closer look.

Implicitly, most people would argue that there is nothing wrong with the use of the word "tribe." It is defined as "a unit of social organization consisting of a number of families, clans, or other groups who share a common ancestry, culture, and leadership." [3] Comparatively, the relevant definitions of "nation" are "A relatively large group of people organized under a single, usually independent government..." and "a people who share common customs, origins, history, and frequently language..." [4]

Now that these two words have been compared one next to the other, there are several things to be noticed. First of all, recognize the sophisticated definition of nation compared to tribe. In the word tribe you have "leadership" and "a unit of social organization," while in nation you have "government." Tribes share simply "ancestry, culture, and leadership," while nations "share common customs, origins, history, and frequently language." If one takes these definitions into account along with a consideration for the frequent condescending tone and context in which people of color are referred to as primitive tribes, a picture begins to develop.

The picture that develops is a subtle use of language, via definition and context, that infers African "tribes" and Native American "tribes" were socially organized and without governance, as opposed to organized in governments with their own hierarchies and ways of managing their own destinies. In this context the use of tribe by Europeans can certainly be explained by the aggressive tendencies of their own culture and their constant insistence on "civilizing and governing" Africans and Native Americans. This use of language can be considered as a subtle justification for these aggressive tendencies.

We should consider our examples of Africans and Native Americans with regard to the nature of these societies prior to European invasion, annihilation and colonization. Certainly Native Americans had government, hierarchy, shared language, customs, origins and history which varied according to the group or nation about which one chooses to speak. For example, the Sioux Nation was very different in many respects from the Iroqouis Nation, but they both were nations by definition. They were much more than units of social organization. In fact, the Iroqouis Nation was an organized federation of six nations of Native Americans. Obviously, tribe is an inadequate descriptor in this case.

While the use of nation to describe Native American peoples is already used currently in a few instances, Africans are almost uniformly referred to as tribes. The Mandinka, Ewe, Yoruba, Kikuyu and the multitude of other Africans are referred to as tribes. This is accepted despite the fact that prior to colonization, these peoples had their own forms of government, hierarchy, customs, origins and still maintain languages specific to the different groups. Moreover, Chancellor Williams, in *The Destruction of Black Civilization*, wrote about the African democratic institutions that developed prior to and without the influence of the West. Much is also known of the great Mali empire of the "Mandinka Nation," the Songhay empire of the "Songhay Nation," Dahomey of the "Fon Nation" and many others. These are a testament to the characterization of these African groups as "nations" by the definitions we have examined.

The Native American and African nations, and their most frequent characterization as tribes, represent very subtle applications of language. However, these are the types of applications of language that we can be pragmatic about analyzing, in addition to the more glaring and obvious examples. The Spanish, Italian, Germans, French, Romanians, Czechoslovakians, etc., are all Europeans on the continent of Europe, but are designated as nations. Similarly the Fon, Kikuyu, Yoruba, etc., are all Africans on the continent of Africa and should be referred to as nations instead of tribes.

With regard to Africa in particular, the classification of the various groups of people as nations seemingly presents a conflict with the already existing nations with their sovereign boundaries. However, it must be kept in mind that the current national boundaries in Africa that separate countries such as Ghana, Togo, Benin and others are a product of European colonialism and are inconsistent with the geography of the nations of people prior to European invasion. It should also be noted that in our use of nation to describe these groups of people, we are referring predominately to language, present or former governmental hierarchies, culture and history. National boundaries do not play a huge role in this context. Therefore, we may still refer to the Mandinka Nation, for example, without conflict with the present nations such as Ghana, Niger, etc. Finally, in all of this we must be practical in our use of language, realizing that in every culture there are nations *and* tribes by definition. We simply must discern for ourselves which is which.

This discussion of language as it relates to the use of words like tribe and nation is just one example of the types of things worthy of *consideration*, especially when we recognize the power of language to define people, mould perceptions, shape attitudes and shape actions. As we return to broader considerations of language we realize that Europeans did not bring "civilization" to native peoples, nor did they "discover" anything. They represented invasion, aggression and decimation to the native peoples who themselves were civilized enough to welcome foreigners to their land.

In today's international political and propaganda arena, Arab Muslims are frequently referred to as "terrorists." When we take a closer look it might be realized that in many instances they are merely defending and fighting for their interests. Where this is the case, they are no more terrorists than Americans or Israelis are in their overt military campaigns against Arab Muslims, or covert CIA and Mossad terrorist activities. Clearly in referring to Muslim activities uniformly as terrorist, public opinion is being shaped to support government policy.

Depending on the circumstances, that government policy may be relating to the control of oil, as was the case in the Persian Gulf War with Sadam Hussein. Sadam Hussein was said to have "invaded" Kuwait. This seems true enough, but we should then question why we hear Israel being referred to not as "invaders," but "occupiers" of Palestinian land. If Israel did not invade, but instead "reclaimed," the land Israel, shouldn't it be said that Iraq "reclaimed" Kuwait if we are factual and equitable, since it was a part of Iraq.

How often is it shared that there was no such place as Israel until 1948 when the war effort to remove Palestinians from their land, by invasion, was finally successful? The claim of European Jews was that the land the Palestinians occupied and lived on was the long lost Jewish homeland according to Biblical prophesy. "Eretz Israel," a term which means "the land of Isreal" in the context of the ancient Jewish land, was the Zionist cry. This was the major basis for the waging of war against the Palestinians to remove them from the land that would become today's Israel. More individuals would be clearer on the current conflict in the Middle East if they knew this history and understood the language.

Though beyond the scope of this chapter and this book, an additional issue in the European Jewish claim to Israel is the question of whether the current European Jews are the Jews of the Bible. This is important since the invasion of Palestinian land was based on Biblical prophesy. There are many who argue that the Jews of the Bible are represented by today's Ethiopian Jews, an African people. Some site the

Bible, specifically Amos 9:7, which states, " 'Are ye not as children of the Ethiopians unto me, O children of Israel?' says the Lord." Language and its use has implications in all of this.

As we move along with our revisitation of language, there are general inconsistencies to point out. Regarding warfare, the reports of "collateral damage" in the Persian Gulf War in real terms means murdered civilians in military operations. Collateral damage is an intentional and palatable manipulation of language fed to the American public, so that the blood of babies and mothers in war doesn't allow the American masses to think about who we go to war with, why and when it is really necessary.

Why are Somalian military leaders "warlords" and "thugs," while Bosnian Serbs are "generals" and "commanding officers?" What does "Third World" mean? We live in one world together and all human life within that world is supposed to be equally valuable. How many of us know that one of the definitions in the 3rd edition of the *American Heritage Dictionary of the English Language* refers to "Minority groups as a whole within a larger prevailing culture" as Third World. [5] Does that mean that when European powers speak in a condescending nature about the Third World they are speaking of Africans in America, not simply the starving, poverty stricken, far away countries of people of color splashed across T.V. screens? Why is it that when you fill out a form that asks you about your race or ethnicity, Italian Americans, German Americans, Irish Americans, and other ethnic/cultural groupings are considered "white," while others, such as Mexican Americans, Alaskan Americans, Pacific Islanders, etc., are considered individually instead of as one group called "people of color?" Africans are usually referred to as Black or African American. Such a classification system may appear as follows:

1) American Indian or Alaskan American
2) Black or African American
3) Mexican, Mexican American, or Chicano
4) Asian, Asian American, or Pacific Islander
5) Puerto Rican
6) Other Hispanic or Latin Americans
7) White (non-Hispanic)
8) Other

* the order and terms used are as they appear on the Graduate Record Examination registration form

On the surface this seems to just confirm our everyday classifications of people. But why are people classified this way?

Certainly, recognizing one's culture is natural. However, another explanation might be that the lumping together of European descendants, into the category of "white," provides for greater numbers in demographic and power considerations. It is a *created* unity, the implications of which ensure that "white" people are considered the majority. Many European Americans identify with their specific homelands and cultural groups, as can be seen in the Sons of Italy, the Irish Caucus, Oktoberfest and many other celebrations and organizations. However, when it comes to counting the numbers the language of power necessitates unity and homogeneity. Therefore, it is very prudent to officially have the cohesion of a "white" category. If we broke the classification of "white" people into their ethnic and national groups, such as Italian, German, English and Irish, they would no longer enjoy the benefits that come along with identifying oneself with the majority.

In reality, such a classification system would be *coherent* and equitable if it read in one of the following two ways:

1) Black/Brown
2) Yellow
3) White
4) Red
5) Other

or

1) Native American or Alaskan Native
2) African, African Caribbean, African South American or African American
3) Mexican, Mexican American, or Chicano
4) Asian, Asian American, or Pacific Islander
5) Puerto Rican
6) Cuban or Cuban American
7) Italian or Italian American
8) Irish or Irish American
9) Spanish or Spanish American
10) German or German American
11) British or British American
12) Korean or Korean American
13) Japanese or Japanese American
14) Chinese or Chinese American
15) Filipino or Filipino American
16) Indian or Indian American

17) Arab or Arab American
18) Russian or Russian American
19) Other

(Both of these classifications are just adaptations of the original classifications and in no way are endorsements of the historical or ideological correctness of any of the three classification models presented.)

This is somewhat complicated and confusing, but often when you come out of the darkness (miseducation and language manipulation) into the light (language understanding and informational empowerment), you squint and may be somewhat disoriented before you adjust to the light.

Why are Africans in America "violent" and "radical" when they speak of freeing themselves from oppression, but George Washington, and Patrick Henry who said "Freedom or Death," are considered "founding fathers" and "heros," even though they waged a bloody Revolutionary War?

These are but few of the issues of language we should be cognizant of. We should also be weary of referring to majority world cultures of color as "non-white" and all other designations that serve to define people with European culture as the point of reference. In other words, define yourself by what *you* are. So, the question becomes whether you will define yourself as "non-white" or as African. It is hoped that the latter would be the choice. Defining yourself and having others define you by a European standard of what you are not (i.e. non-white) doesn't ever have to be the case because it is elitist, arrogant, and assigns various world cultures to peripheral status as "other" in relation to the European standard.

The crafty use of language has been a part of Western oppression for years. When America was speaking of the "land of the free and home of the brave," Africans were slaves, Native Americans had been decimated, and people, including members of those oppressed groups, were still singing the songs. This is psychological warfare of the type that has been so successful in making many of us believe that America holds African people in high enough esteem to include them in their grandiose rhetoric. The unfortunate fact is that the language of freedom and justice has always been a facade in America and throughout the world where people have been oppressed; but as in so many other instances, America controls the definitions and they control the people who accept them.

African people must learn to define themselves. If we are to use the English language, which many in the world do, we must use it well. It isn't even a matter of "trying to sound white." It is a matter of speaking whatever language you choose to speak well enough to harness the tremendous power of the spoken word. It is also a matter of being proficient enough with language to see when it is being used against you.

If we are to use language and recognize that it is a tool, we must use it properly in order to gain any benefit. An individual who has a hammer and doesn't know how to use it, is helpless to build anything. In fact, if that individual attempts to use that hammer he or she might injure himself or herself. The same is true with language. If you intend to operate in the United States, with the majority of African people speaking English, you are helpless to build a movement if you don't know how to use the language. One doesn't have to speak "the King's" English, but must know how to use it as a tool. Those of us who don't know how to use it hurt ourselves when we accept the defintions that others give us for ourselves. On the other hand, Brother Malcolm X (El Haaj Malik El Shabaaz) knew how to use the tool of language. Dr. Martin Luther King new how to use language. The Honorable Minister Louis Farrakhan knows how to use language. The masses don't have to be as eloquent as these brothers. They must be simply aware of the language they speak and are defined by.

Kujichagulia (Koo-je-cha-gu-lia), **Self-determination***. to define ourselves, name ourselves, create for ourselves and speak for ourselves instead of being defined, named, created for and spoken for by others.*

Chapter 9

PAWNS IN POPULATION POLITICS

In the book, *Awaken*, there was a short chapter entitled "Africa: The Pawn." Included in that chapter was reference to the issue of world population growth and the reaction of the U.N. and the West in general. It was mentioned that the U.N. had done a report on population growth and possible future resource catastrophes, sounding the alarm to slow growth in Africa, South Asia, and Latin America, with emphasis on "education and family planning." There was also some mention of the natural resources that are exploited from these continents by "industrialized" nations, as has been discussed in this book, and essentially means that Europe and America both exploit the resources taken from Africa, South America, and South Asia. These resources that should be going to the people are being pillaged, causing many of the conditions of poverty, famine and political instability. Our discussion of colonialism reflects this.

Now a few years have passed and the issue of population intensifies by leaps and bounds. Articles flood the nation's newspapers with titles such as "Third World Horrors: Sign of Scarcity?: Experts Split on Role of Population Growth." [1] This article places population in the specter of being a cause of the events of Haitian turmoil and the Rwanda tragedy. The article mentions the United Nations conference that was held in September 1993 in Cairo, Egypt and outlines the intentions of the United States and other countries to step in and stabilize population problems.

For the conscious reader this article contradicts itself by assigning population growth the blame for conflict, famine and poverty in "developing" nations. Two statements in particular from this article highlight the contradiction. The first claims that "Indeed, demographers predict that 95 percent of the world's population growth will occur in developing countries that are probably least able to support it, in Africa, Latin America and Asia." [2] Incidentally all of these "developing" countries are former European colonies still controlled by their colonizers. We have outlined Africa in this book, the Spanish and Portuguese dominated South America, and the British ravaged South Asia or India. However, these facts are not needed to see why these countries and continents suffer as they do, because the very same article gives us some insight. It goes on to say that:

> In terms of environmental impact, Americans and other citizens of the industrialized world consume far more resources per person, and produce far more waste and pollution, than their poorer neighbors. The one-fifth of the world population living in developed countries consumes two-thirds of all resources and generates 75 percent of the wastes, environmentalists note. [3]

It is right there in black and white so that one does not even have to read between the lines! Why then is the solution proposed as curbing the population of these "developing " countries, instead of as ceasing to exploit the people and the land, which would allow them to develop and sustain themselves? Why not curb developed countries' resource use and waste production? The only reason these "developing" countries cannot support their population is because their resources are under siege and their people are oppressed.

Still other articles have appeared in various publications including *U.S.A. Today*. One such article by Margaret Usdansky that occupies the front page of the August 31, 1994 edition of *U.S.A Today*, is lead by a headline that reads in bold red letters "Population Peril," and is entitled "Birth control, abortion are tough issues." Though this article addresses the specific issue of whether or not abortion will play an official role in population control, which is a big issue, it still contains statements like the following:

> Though population growth alone is not responsible for the world's calamities, there is growing agreement that it is an important contributing factor.
> Look at almost any country plagued by civil strife, says Atwood. "You see abject poverty, high population growth rates, environmental degradation, food shortages. These are the conditions that contribute to the growth of extremists." [4]

What about the role of colonialism, resource exploitation and oppression in causing all of these conditions and necessitating, not extremism, but justifiable resistance and reactionary conflict? Again, there is the conspicuous absence of an examination of the real causes of the existing conditions. This silence can correctly be attributed to both guilt, continuing hidden agendas and ulterior motives, because we take for granted that the West* is intelligent enough not to miss such obvious pieces of the puzzle.

Another article in the very same edition of *U.S.A. Today* is entitled "Africa's quandary: More people, less food." [5] This article is yet another population charade that begins by saying "Nowhere in the world do population growth and food shortages crunch together to create such widespread misery as in Africa." Why is it not recognized that if whole African countries did not have 80-90 percent of their land being used by outsiders to produce cash crops and commodities that neither sustain the lives of the rightful owners of the land nor provide them wealth, conditions would be very different today? They could be different tomorrow if the world were interested in real solutions.

Of course people would still have some problems, just as the United States and other "industrialized" countries suffer from earthquakes, hurricanes, crime, poverty, poor health and so on. But one must know that neither Africa nor any other place in the world is better off as a result of the European world presence and their white world supremacy. It must be called what it is, especially in the face of this huge campaign to cover the crimes of inhumanity, exploitation and oppression with cries of population growth. Africa, India and Latin America are in their present condition precisely because of those who are now pretending that they know nothing beyond the fact that population is causing these problems.

As we see, the framework is being laid for the West to increase its strangle hold on Africa, her people, other people of color and their lands. It is upon us to achieve some degree of political consciousness, sophistication and self determination. This is so because, not only will Africans become expendable and scientifically brutalized on the continent, but their expendability is our expendability. Scientific brutalization is another subject all together. In *Awaken*, questions were posed about AIDS proliferation in Africa and its decimation of major portions of the population. We have seen in the latest population debates, even in the articles outlined above, that mass government sponsored abortion projects are being talked about as a solution. And, in *Black Africa: The Economic and Cultural Basis for a Federated State* by Chiekh Anta Diop, there was discussion of U.S. plans in the seventies to control population via putting sterilizing agents into water supplies and the salt of target populations. These things constitute scientific brutalization. We must wake up.

We have already spoken in great depth about our necessary unity in this book. Our need for global political consciousness is unquestionable and must accompany a more sophisticated understanding of the political machine as it operates in the U.S.

*We use the term "West" repeatedly as a reference to Europe and the U.S.

CHAPTER 10

DRUMS FROM THE HILLS: REVOLUTION & RECLAMATION IN MUSIC

> Music is sacred. It is an integral part of the Way of Life of
> many traditional cultures throughout the world; it is the invocation of
> vital energies that ensure a community's survival.
>   Sule Greg Wilson, <u>The Drummer's Path:</u>
>   <u>Moving the Spirit with Ritual and</u>
>   <u>Traditional Drumming</u>

The rythyms of percussion that are characteristic of African
culture have always had, and continue to have, a significant impact on
spirituality and continued struggle. At the genesis of the Haitian
Revolution the Voodoo priest, Boukman, called his fellow Africans of Haiti
to the hills with the drums. The drums of Africa "speak" to those who will
listen. This is manifested in specific rythyms actually used to
communicate or relay messages (as in the Haitian Revolution), as well as
the way in which the drums tend to even stir things inside of the person
who casually listens to music and finds themselves bopping their head to
the strong beats, without conscious thought of their movement. This is
part of what we retained, despite the Great Suffering, of our collective
cultural and spiritual consciousness.

In African descended spiritual traditions such as Candomblé,
Santería and Voodoo, the drums take on a sacred role of calling the orishas
from their home in Africa to manifest for and in the spiritual
communities. Individual orishas such as Shango, Oshun or Oya will have

specific drum rythyms dedicated to them and specific to them.

In a similar manner, the drum beats in particular, and more importantly the music and lyrics in general, are elements of rap music which call us to consciousness, spirituality and action. In this chapter we want to examine the parallels between rap music and the drums of revolution, spirituality and cultural reclamation that issued the call to brothers and sisters in revolutions such as that in Haiti.

As an art form, rap music is very diverse, healthy and mostly positive in the sense that it often expresses and deals with the painful realities of our communities or simply provides good entertainment. The element of rap that draws parallels to the drums of revolution and reclamation is an incredibly complex, conscious, cultural, political music form. Artists such as Arrested Development, Poor Righteous Teachers, X-Clan, KRS-One, Paris, Queen Latifah, Public Enemy and many others make up this element, which itself is diverse beyond the abiltity to categorize or label it. These artists, in their own varying ways, are playing the role of the drums of Boukman in Haiti. They are calling their listeners, who are more than disenfranchised youth, to consciousness and resistance. This may be why rap has been tagged as a negative, homogenous entity. The stigma of negativity has been given based on the misdirected and exploited actions of a segment of rappers whose trivial and negative   images have been made popular by the media and money hungry record companies; this is not to mention those of us who perpetuate the popularity of the negative side of the art by purchasing tapes, CD's and concert tickets. All the while, the positive, uplifting, conscious, revolutionary rap music is effectively overshadowed and/or lumped into the negative image of rap. This is an effective means of minimalizing its impact.

We can look specifically at the overlooked and de-emphasized importance of some of these artists by examining how they "speak" to us through their lyrics and their rythyms. A particularly positive, spiritual and culturally grounded group like Arrested Development is a good place to start. This group has managed to get some "mainstream" attention, but their importance goes far beyond the "mainstream" attraction to their unique sound.

On the surface one can look at the outward appearance and vibe of the group. The many members in African locks and other natural hairstyles, African clothing and varying hues of beautiful blackness are a manifestation of what they represent. The rythyms that they offer are also strongly African, especially on cuts such as the short interlude called "The Drum" on their latest recording, *Zingalamaduni*. "The Drum" is one minute and fifty-seven seconds of African drumming which starts as an almost distant sound and builds to a powerful crescendo before moving into the next song.

Often times the music and the vibes of a group are heard and felt by listeners more prominently than the lyrics, but with Arrested Development what they have to say to us in their lyrics is also extremely important. Not only have they "called us to the hills" with their rythyms, but on cuts like "Africa's inside me," they speak about the spirit and cultural roots of Africa that remain inside of us all. The leader of the group, Speech, exclaims that "Africa's a boiling over flowing inside of me" [1] and the hook, or chorus, proclaims that:

> Africa's inside of me
> taking back her child
> she's giving me my pride
> and setting me free. [2]

This is reclamation and cultural revolution in the music of Arrested Development. This is the memory of the Great Suffering. This is Boukman, David Walker or Marcus Garvey in the midst of today's youth and adults who enjoy the positive and uplifting message manifested in rap music. In another of the songs, entitled "Ease My Mind," on the *Zingalamaduni* recording, Speech informs us that he moves:

> ... with confidence of harmony
> and do my thang to resist this wack society.
> Cuz if you don't resist, & I mean consciously
> you'll fool your subconscious into accepting it.
> I ain't acceptin'. I keep my focus. [3]

If in the music of Arrested Development we are drawn to the rythyms, this example shows that we are nourished with the spirit of resistance by the lyrics once we are pulled in by the beats. We as a people cannot fail to properly acknowledge the power of rap music, whether we personally enjoy it or not. In an article in YSB (Young Sisters & Brothers) magazine, Speech is described as an Africanist and qouted as saying "I just wish African people realized we had real power, worldwide-from Brazil, to Africa, Europe and the Caribbean." [4] This is a powerfully conscious attitude being expounded by a brother and a group that expresses themselves through one of the most powerful mediums in the world: music.

As a group, Arrested Development contributes a significant component to our struggle as Speech communicates through strong and moving lyrics, with his African locks cascading; Montsho-Eshe dances to the African rythyms and displays the beauty of the African woman; Baba

OJE provides the spirit and wisdom of an elder; and other members, such as Headliner, Nadirah Shakoor, Rasa Don, Ajile, Kwesi Asuo and Aerle Taree provide dancing, beats, rythyms, vocals and the spirit of Arrested Developmemt.

Positivity in the form of cultural and political consciousness is not a rare or unusual phenomenon in rap music. Arrested Development is a single example to be complemented by numerous others. KRS-One is another example of this type of revolutionary enlightenment through music. He has been a consistent voice of consciousness. The title of one of his collections of recordings is *Edutainment*. This title implies the dual role of the music produced by KRS-One as being both entertaining and educational. He refers to his own work on *Edutainment* as "educational rap on a militant revolutionary level."[5] On a song by KRS-One entitled "Why is That?," the lyrics let us know that:

> The day of the ignorant rapper is done
> knowledge reigns supreme of nearly everyone.[6]

It is in fact said that KRS-One stands for "**K**nowledge **R**eigns **S**upreme **O**ver **N**early **E**veryone." One cannot help feeling in an artist like KRS-One, and in his music, the power of the African drums for which this chapter is named. It is the draw of the rythym and the mental nourishment of consciousness and revolution.

An interlude on *Edutainment,* called Exhibit A, which is in the form of a lecture, gives yet another example of the powerful impact and philosophy of KRS-One.

> Rap music, what does it mean? What is everybody in this industry for? What is everybody buying rap for? Why do people get involved in rap music? Rap music, number one, is the voice of Black people, number one. Number two, it's the last voice of Black people. Black people have created every music you hear out here in the streets today... Therefore, in a situation that has all African music in it... all African influence in all its music, and you have what is called American Music Awards, you have what is called theft. And what I would like to bring out today is rap music as a revolutionary tool in changing the structure of racist America.[7]

The beginning of the song that follows is an exhortation by KRS-One to "Wake up! Take the pillow from your head, and put a book in!"[8] To back up this exhortation, KRS-One proceeds to give lessons in his lyrics that would make anyone not aware of the information go and look it up. He "teaches" African history, religion, contemporary issues and host of other subjects.

On the level of African culture and teaching through lyrics, X-Clan is a group immersed in it from their appearance to the mind state they present on their albums. The complex lyrics are often not understood by listeners who don't study them. Yes, much like a book, the lyrics of X-Clan must be studied to gain the "full" meaning. They are filled with the knowledge of Kemet, Yoruba spirituality, the Great Suffering and the consciousness of African struggle. Songs from their album, *To The East Blackwards*, give us examples. In the song "Funkin' Lesson" we hear Brother J declare, "Onward ride as I talk of Ra, coverse with Horus, create with Ptah, I rock to Geb, to war with Bas..."[9] Grand Verbalizer Funkin' Lesson Brother J is speaking of ancient Kemet here. Ra is God symbolized by the sun. Horus is the son of God, often represented by a Falcon and bearing titles like Prince of Peace and Light of the World. Ptah is the "God force" or manifestation of God which represents creation, mind and thought, among other things. Geb is the God force manifested as the Earth. And, Bas or Bast, symbolized by a cat, represents the power of the Sun (God). These are not mere ryhmes about any silly subject, as many people believe all rap to be. It just so happens that the popular media and record companies pay much more attention to the purely entertaining rap and the degrading rap.

In the same song, "Funkin' Lesson," Professor X proclaims, "Yes it gets blacker, with a Nat Turner lick. Martin, Adam, Malcolm, Huey... there's a party at the crossroads."[10] This is a sample of more political and historical consciousness. In the song, "Grand Verbalizer, What Time Is It?," Brother J gives us more of the cultural orientation when he begins his flow by responding to the chorus saying that the time is "African, very African. Come and step in brother's temple, see what's happening."[11] There is no question as to how X-Clan defines themselves as to who they are and from where they have come. In a song called "Tribal Jam," Brother J relates that he's

> Quite illogical but never been a savage, genes scientific but I never have to map it.
> I'm harder than the diamond that the eater might steal.
> I'm never mythical, divinity is real.
> Mind state still ever stable to the end, nations begin
> BlackWatch will defend.
> So now you raise the flag of the blood race earth.
> Freedom or death and death unto birth, we carry on.[12]

The lyrics of X-Clan only get deeper and accentuate the creative power of this rap and its relevance to our lives and struggle. To accompany their lyrics, X-Clan dresses in their African clothing and choose to adorn their bodies with golden (and sometimes other metals with spiritual significance) rings in their ears, noses and on their fingers. With all of this, their songs are put to music that drops beats and samples that could compete with *any* rap music for the ears of our young.

Chuck D of Public Enemy is another of the rappers that teaches through his music. The song "Fight the Power" is a well known example of the mood of resistance in Public Enemy's music. Coupled with this resistence is enlightenment. The lyrics of Chuck D have introduced many youngsters, and the not so young, to the Honorable Minister Louis Farrakhan. On *Fear Of A Black Planet*, Public Enemy speaks indirectly of Dr. Francis Cress Welsing's Theory of Color Confrontation in both the title of this album and the song that bears the same name.

Of the songs on this album, "Fight the Power" is one that mobilized the masses of African youth into conscious thought about our condition as an oppressed people. "Fight the Power" became a slogan and a rallying cry for the younger generation in the late eighties. It is on this song that Chuck D proclaims in his rapid, hard style, "My beloved, let's get down to business, mental self-defense or fitness." [13]

Fear Of A Black Planet bears the phrase "The Counterattack on World Supremacy..." on the cover. Another release of Public Enemy, entitled *Apocalypse 91... The Enemy Strikes Black*, bears the phrase "Justice Evolves Only After Injustice Is Defeated." On the inside cover of their latest album, *Muse Sick-N-Hour Mess Age*, there is a message from Chuck D. A quote from that message captures the essence of Chuck D and the other rappers of this cultural and political element of rap.

> Perhaps this is the unavoidable outcome of a racist blueprint, that Black America eats itself...
> People have the nerve to blame rap music for this process, when it may just be our last cry for help. As, today wars are fought in the air, call these records air-strikes from the airwaves. [14]

We have taken a look at only a few of the rappers who contribute significantly to our consciousness, identity and continued struggle. All of this has been to say that this form of expression, rap, is not simply the trifle of confused and rebellious teens. In some of the rap music that our brothers and sisters are producing, there is a strong resemblence to the call of the drums that have spurred us to revolution, resistance, spirituality and communication throughout our history.

The resemblence doesn't end with the music and its effect on the listener. Rap is under attack, much like the drums of old. Perhaps the focus is said to be on negative rap and "gangsta" rap, but the entire art is continuosly slandered while the positives of it are ignored. (The exception here is when rap is used commercially as an exploited art form for profit. There are few commercials for cereals, toys, fast food, etc. that do not have some form of rap to aid in the sale of the product. In this arena rap is not ignored or slandered. Profit has priority.)

Even with regard to some of the rap that is viewed as negative because of harsh language and innuendos of violent lifestyles; not the groups with a sort of manufactured, commercial "gangsta" sexism and profanity, there is something we must keep in mind. If we accept the fact that in a very real sense we as a people are at war, we must realize that war is not always sane nor are its victims/participants always cloaked in the garment of clearly articulated, focused warfare. Sometimes victims/participants in war simply fight in any way they can. This may be manifested in confusion, dismal outlooks, rebellion and sometimes negativity. These are the casualties of war and some of our young people who are rapping may fall into this category as they express their condition.

It is not for us to condone negative behavior, only come to an understanding of it so that we might correct it amongst our people. With this said, we can conclude by refocusing our attention on the brothers and sisters who are producing the rythyms of consciousness and resistence. They are under attack in as much as rap in general is under attack and they are not fully acknowledged as a valuable entity within rap. This attack is reminiscent of what was taking place with European attitudes towards the rythyms and effects of the drums during the Maafa, as described by Sule Greg Wilson.

> In South Carolina they lived with it and feared it. They experienced the power of the Spirit-calling drum. That's why in 1740, after the Stono Rebellion, the South Carolina colonial assembly outlawed hand drums... With the across-the-miles communication that talking drums gave Africans, those who rose up against slavery and utilized that technology stood a good chance of success. To destroy that military power, Europeans said drums-all drums-had to stop. The law was: You play, you lose your hand. Maryland, then other colonies, quickly followed suit with similar "no-drumming-in-public" laws. [15]

Do we hear the young brother and sister warriors of rap music or only the knuckleheads that the record companies love to make "more gangsta" for profit? Doesn't someone have to listen to music for it to be popular? Do we hear our young warriors? We have a tremendous resource for liberation in the consciousness of the cultural and political rappers. They are the drums from the hills for many.

PART IV
HEALING TIME

CHAPTER 11

PSYCHOLOGICAL TRAGEDY: SCARS OF THE MAAFA

One sad reality that cannot be overlooked in dealing with the Maafa is the lasting psychological effect that the Maafa has had on all people. Yes, African people speak of the miseducation and brainwashing that we have received, but it goes deeper than that. Europeans and all who have been engulfed by Western culture have suffered psychologically in one way or another. It must be realized that European or white world supremacy, grounded in racism, is the framework in which most of the world operates. The United States and Europe currently exercise their cultural and economic influence over the world. Consequently, the world has fallen under the influence of people who built their power on the kidnapping, rape, murder, brutalization and psychological battering of African people. This fact of history carries dual consequences. The obvious consequence is the psychological damage done to African people over hundreds of years. The other very real consequence is that the minds of the masses of Europeans had to be molded, twisted and manipulated to particpate in and perpetuate the heinous crimes of humanity. In addition, those people who consciously warped, and continue to warp, the minds of others into racism and barbarity are themselves psychologically troubled to a completely different level.

The Great Suffering has dictated that African people come through an experience that is traumatic beyond belief. As a psychologist, Na'im Akbar shares the following:

> The slavery that captures the mind and incarcerates the
> motivation, perception, aspiration, and identity in a web of anti-self
> images, generating a personal and collective self-destruction, is more
> cruel than the shackles on the wrists and ankles. The slavery that
> feeds on the psychology, invading the soul of man, destroying his
> loyalties to himself and establishing allegiance to forces which destroy
> him, is an even worse capture. The influences that permit an illusion
> of freedom, liberation, and self-determination, while tenaciously

holding one's mind in subjugation, is the folly of only the sadistic. [1]

The profound observations of Dr. Akbar touch on three very important areas worthy of examination. These areas are:

1) The psychological damage that the Maafa has done to African people. Psychologically, the inflicted damage is on the one hand from the pure trauma of witnessing and suffering the intense physical abuse. On the other hand, psychological war fare was waged by intentional mental abuse, misinformation, miseducation, etc.
2) The psychological impact that the Maafa has had on Europeans who have participated in its racist legacy.
3) The sickness of individuals who consciously manipulated the minds of their European contemporaries to enthusiastically participate in the Maafa, as well as the sickness of those who continue to perpetuate these mind states.

From the perspective of the Africans who suffered through the Maafa, the mere thought of *lifetimes* of dehumanization, physical brutality and rape is painful to think about. The physical toil and abuse was devastating. For example, children had to watch their mothers being raped. Consider the scars that this leaves on a child. As impressionable as children are, for a child to watch or hear a parent being raped has to leave an emotional imprint in the memory that is damaging for a lifetime. One also must know the trauma a woman suffers through when she is raped.

Psychologic assessment: Rape presents both psychological and social problems for the victims, who must handle their own feelings as well as face the often negative reactions (eg, judgemental, derisive) of friends, family, and officials. Patients should be viewed as undergoing a **posttraumatic stress disorder** that typically has an *acute phase* lasting a few days to a few weeks, followed by a *long-term process* of reorganization and recovery.

Acute phase reactions are fear and anger, although patients outward responses range from talkativeness, tenseness, crying, and trembling to shock and disbelief, with dispassion, quiescence, and smiling. The latter responses are rarely an indication that the patient is unconcerned; they may be avoidance reactions or may occur in patients who have coping styles that require control of emotion or who are physically exhausted. Patients are usually severely frightened and embarrassed and feel degraded. The anger felt by many victims may be displaced onto hospital personnel, who should be aware of this and not troubled by it

Long-range effects of rape include reexperiencing the assault, aversion to sex, anxiety, phobias, suspiciousness, depression, night mares and sleep disorders, somatic symptoms, and social withdrawal. [2]

The severity of a rape experience should be apparent as it is related to us by the well respected Merck Manual of Diagnosis and Therapy. Our African sisters had to deal not just with the single harmful experience of being raped, but were repeatedly and randomly raped by ravenous enslavers. As far as treatment for rape is concerned, "the psychological aspects are the most potentially damaging and require sophisticated management. It is very important to treat patients with respect, to see that they are not left alone, to assure them that they are safe, to demonstrate understanding and empathy..." [3]

Given the circumstances of the Maafa, the rape victims had no time to heal, nor was treatment readily available. The African man, regardless of the respect that he might attempt to show to the woman, could not assure her that she was safe. It would have also been very difficult for him or anyone else to demonstrate understanding in the madness and confusion of the Maafa.

Additionally, husbands had to watch the repeated sexual abuse of their wives and fathers watched the repeated rape of their daughters. This had to be an emasculating experience. The aspect of manhood defined by one's ability to protect his family was taken away.

There was also the agony of watching loved ones suffer the excruciating pain of the whip, not to mention the mind numbing experience of being beaten. In addition, Africans were often times forced to beat their own brothers and sisters to spare themselves.

The Great Suffering represented hundreds of years of torture. Individual Africans lived their entire lives being tortured. One is hard pressed to even conceive of all of the forms of physical torture. There where the thumbscrews, brands, whips, shackles, mutilation, rape and the list continues on and on. It is amazing that African people are not a completely broken people.

If one looks at the effects of torture in prisoners of war who are freed and return home, they often suffer from nightmares, flashbacks, physical disabilities and sometimes insanity. In fact, this is often the case for people who have participated in war with simply being in combat representing their only torture. Posttraumatic Stress Disorder is what commonly affects these war veterans.

If the barbarity and trauma of war can do so much damage to the mind, we can only imagine what damage must have been done from life-times and generations of intense suffering during the Maafa. Posttraumatic Stress Disorder is defined as "A neurotic disorder produced by exposure to an overwhelming environmental stress..." [4] Given this defintion, it should be clear that a closer look at Posttraumatic Stress Disorder might give us further insight into the detrimental effects of the Great Suffering.

> The etiologic sine qua non of the disorder is exposure to an overwhelming environmental stress. Since not every individual responds to such stress with a posttraumatic stress syndrome, a variety of factors in clinical combination are required to produce the pathological state. These include (1) the suddenness and unexpected-ness of the stress, as in major fires, explosions, and airplane crashes, or in natural disasters like floods, earthquakes, and tornadoes; (2) the bloody brutality and horror of events associated with active armed combat or terrorist attacks; (3) the more prolonged and chronic stress of exposure to inhumane treatment such as occurs in POW and concentration camps, with the frequently associated torture and atrocities; (4) the psychologic and constitutional strengths and weaknesses of the victim; (5) concurrent bodily injury (especially of the head) suffered by the victim; and (6) the nature and availability of social supports. [5]

The applicability of Posttraumatic Stress Disorder to African people and the Maafa is striking. The Maafa more than qualifies as *the* over-whelming environmental stress. In fact, it is extremely informative to rewrite the etiology of Posttraumatic Stress Disorder using the Maafa as the specific experience causing onset. Such a rewritten defintion might appear as follows:

> The etiological sin qua non of the disorder is exposure to the stress of the Maafa. Since not every individual responds to such stress with posttraumatic stress syndrome, a variety of factors in clinical combination are required to produce the pathologic state. These include (1) the suddenness and unex-pectedness of being kidnapped and separated from family and friends, as in the Maafa for the Africans who came directly from the continent; (2) the bloody brutality and horror of events associated with the Maafa; (3) the more prolonged and chronic

stress of exposure to inhumane treatment such as was a way of life to those who were unable to gain freedom or escape, and consequently endured torture and atrocities (It should be noted that even free Africans were subjected to inhumane treatment.); (4) the psychological and constitutional strengths and weaknesses of the Africans who suffered through the Maafa; (5) concurrent bodily injury (especially whippings, rape and mutilations) suffered by the victim; and (6) the nature and availability of social supports or the nature of continued, intense and persistent stress.

Compare this rewriting of the etiology of Posttraumatic Stress Disorder with the actual etiology and it is stunning how well the Maafa qualifies to be a cause of this disorder. If anything, Posttraumatic Stress Disorder might not be quite sufficient to capture the psychological damage of the Maafa. The signs and symptoms, such as impairment of memory, chronic anxiety, phobic reaction to remembrance, emotional lability, emotional death, hyperalertness, detachment and irritability are all documentable in the experience of many Africans of the Maafa and, in fact, witnessable in many Africans of the present.

Given this history of the Maafa and its psychological implications, it would be helpful to look at what the treatment recommendations are for the disorder.

> Treatment is aimed largely at relieving the prominent hyperarousal and anxiety symptoms. Behavioral desensitization and relaxation techniques are particularly helpful, and where dissociative mechanisms underlie symptom formation, psychotherapy aimed at catharsis, abreaction, and insight may be useful. [6]

As we address treatment in relation to the stress of the Maafa, it might be helpful to define some of the terms used in the above qoutation. *Catharsis* means "A release of emotional tension, as after an overwhelming experience, that restores or refreshes the spirit" and "A technique used to relieve tension and anxiety by bringing repressed feelings and fears to consciousness." [7] What we have here is psychology and medicine affirming that in order to get over the harmful effects of the Maafa, the experience needs to be brought to the consciousness of those affected by it. Abreaction is "to release (repressed emotions) by acting out, as in words, behavior, or the imagination, the situation causing conflict." [8]

For African people, the psychological damage the "environmental stress" of the Maafa caused has been done. This book and its dealing with the Maafa is part of the treatment for the mental states that many of us are still burdened with. Unfortunately, the masses of African people have received no treatment at all and act out behaviors that by all indicators could be classified as insane.

While the extent of our ill health due to psychological stress can only be imagined, what is not left to our imagination is that some of the effects of this dehumanization and physical torture manifest themselves today in the lives of African people. The fear and sense of helplessness that leads many African people to inactivity in the struggle for liberation is quite probably a remnant of the physical brutality and punishment endured by our ancestors. If a mother and father exhibit abnormal or negative behaviors throughout their lifetime , their children will likely pick up these behaviors and, under the same horrid conditions, keep these behaviors while passing them to the generations to follow. Fear is one such behavior.

Even today many of our brothers and sisters would prefer to de-bate why African people cannot be self-determined rather than speak of what we can do towards that end. Instead of looking for solutions, these individuals will devote their energies to convincing those who fight for liberation that it is not possible. We find ourselves shunning the memory of the Maafa as a people and slipping into denial when it comes to dealing with these painful events. Many of our youth and adults demonstrate emotional death in their callous disregard for their own lives and the lives of others, as they kill one another unmercifully.

As tragic as this trauma may seem on its own, we must add the direct psychological warfare and mental abuse perpetrated against African people to what has already been discussed. Lerone Bennett spoke to this aspect of psychological damage when he wrote:

> Slavery was characterized by systematic brainwashing. Slaves were taught to hate themselves and stand in fear of every white man. Every medium was used to detach them from prior sanctions and to flatten their perception and instincts. There is an extremely percep-tive remark on this point in Alexis de Tocqueville's study of America. Said he: "The only means by which the ancients maintained their slavery were fetters and death; the Americans of the South of the Union have discovered more intellectual securities for the duration of their power. They have employed their despotism and their violence against the human mind." [9]

"Violence against the mind" is what taught African people that coarse hair is "bad" hair, wide African noses are ugly, beautiful skin shades of black and brown are unsavory, full lips are unattractive and that

African people are both aesthetically and genetically inferior. Many of our people bought into this miseducation and brainwashing process that has been passed from generation to generation. This is what precipitated the results of a study in which African children preferred European dolls to African dolls, thinking that the African dolls were ugly and bad compared to the beautiful and good European dolls. This is the damage that causes children to make fun of the darkest child or allows adults to use terms like "pickaninny" and "buckwheat" to refer to those of their brothers and sisters who wear their hair in natural styles like African Locks. It is sad to see African people reject themselves, which is particularly evident in the way they treat others like them.

Perhaps more damaging than the negative images of ourselves that have been shown to us is in all forms of media, the European academic community has played a major role in our miseducation and brainwashing. This is a product of the Maafa from the standpoint that many theories of inferiority and subhuman character were crafted about African people in order to justify the Maafa. Consequently, African people were subjected to an indoctrination process in American education that told them they were inferior based on science. To illustrate their point Europeans pointed to the degraded status of African people, used the Bible to convince us that our lot in life was to be servile and obedient, and falsified history to make African people believe they had contributed nothing to civilization and, in fact, had no history to speak of. There was also the type of brainwashing that manipulated and divided African people according to such trifles as age, sex, skin color, hair texture, etc. (See the beginning of Chapter 3 for Willie Lynch qoute.)

Carter G. Woodson addressed these problems in *The Mis-Education of the Negro*. Woodson's focus was primarily on education and schooling, but his points are cogent with regard to the mental violence of academia against African people.

> In geography the races were described in conformity with the program of the usual propaganda to engender in whites a race hate of the Negro, and in the Negroes contempt for themselves. [10]

Woodson went on to describe the miseducation of Africans and Europeans in the various disciplines. He illuminated the aspects of curriculum that depicted African people as fit only to serve others because of their lower order humanity. According to Woodson, even medical schools reminded Africans that they carried germs and nasty diseases like animals, marking their inferior nature. This type of pseudo-science was a carry over from the Maafa as a justification for it.

It is quite easy to see the psychological abuse that the Maafa has caused African people. Again, very few of us have undergone any treatment or therapy to get over these psychological scars. In fact, as Dr. Akbar mentioned in the qoute cited at the beginning of this chapter, there are influences that allow the illusion of liberation amongst African people. This makes the work of those who would struggle for true liberation that much more difficult, because many of their fellow sufferers don't realize the extent of their suffering.

As one looks at the mental illness that the Maafa has caused, the problem does not lie solely with African people. It is important to examine the psychological problems of European Americans. As Woodson pointed out, in the area of education Europeans left the process with miseducated attitudes about themselves and African people. In a book called *The Black Image in the White Mind*, it is said that:

> Pseudoscientific racism or its equivalent tended during the period of this study to increase its hold on the American mind and to infect even those whites who resist its full implications.[11]

The reason that this is of some importance here is because the majority of African people are still subjected to the attitudes, pyschological trauma and, in some cases, insanity of Europeans. This is largely due to the fact that the institutions that are in place around the world are directly descended from or are the same institutions that existed during the Maafa. These institutions, established by Europeans, are the places where the masses of African people receive their education, bank, shop, receive information and participate in numerous other of life's activities. For this reason the attitudes and psychological profiles of these institutions and the people who perpetuate them, Europeans, are worth examination. Also, the examination of the psychosis of Europeans affords us further opportunity to concommitantly address the direct psychological damage that European psychosis has had on African people.

One question that must be asked is, "what drives the minds of a collective group of people to brutally and systematically murder, miseducate, subjugate and psychologically batter others?" The same amount of energy has not been devoted to the study of the collective European psyche as has been devoted to the African, however, three definitions for particular personality disorders might be mentioned to stimulate thought.

Paranoid personalities are characterized by projection of their own conflicts and hostilities onto others (see also Ch. 143). These persons are markedly sensitive in interpersonal relationships and tend to find hostile and malevolent intentions behind trivial, innocent, or even kindly acts by others. Often their suspicious attitudes lead to aggressive feelings or behavior or bring about rejection by others, which seems to justify their original feelings; however, they are unable to see their own roles in this cycle. Their behavior may be designed to prove their adequacy, while their sense of superiority becomes exxagerated and is accompanied by belittlement of others. In many spheres these persons may be highly efficient and conscientious, although envious and inflexible. They may be litiguous, especially when they feel a sense of righteous indignation. [12]

Without even going into a detailed comparison, parallels between the actions of Europeans and Paranoid personalities are apparent. The history of the Maafa clearly shows that Europeans have exhibited any number of these behaviors as a group. Exxagerated sense of superiority and belittlement of others manifests in such things as the European claim to the highest level of civilization, accompanied by the espousal of pseudo-scientific theorems concerning the inferiority of African people serving to justify enslavement and oppression.

More specifically, one can look at instances such as that of Henry Breasted, an acclaimed Egyptologist, claiming that the glorious African civilization of ancient Kemet (Egypt) was comprised of a "Great White Race," as evidence of an exxagerated sense of superiority. Or, one can see exxagerated senses of superiority that manifest in the commentary of European historians like Aurthur Schlesinger when they state:

> ... whatever the crimes of Europe, that continent is also the source-- the *unique* source--of those liberating ideas of individual liberty, political democracy, the rule of law, human rights and cultural freedom that constitute our most precious legacy and to which most of the world today aspires. These are *European* ideas, not Asian, nor African, nor Middle Eastern ideas, except by adoption. [13]

Statements of inaccurate arrogance like this one from a man well respected by the European "mainstream" are not uncommon. This is the type of thinking that has also found its way into acceptance in American educational texts and pedagogical approaches, further damaging and belittling Africans, and others, who are unfortunate enough to accept it as truth. The belittling of others also takes more direct form. *The Bell Curve*, for example, makes a flimsy attempt to show the genetic inferiority suffered by African people in the area of intelligence. This book is a 1994 replay of a recurrent theme that Europeans bring up every ten years or so, with stunning consistency over long periods of time.

If we briefly trace some variants on the same theme, we can see Michael Levin, Ph.D., a professor at the City University of New York, expounding a belief of inferior African intelligence on nationally televised talk shows in the early 90's; Aurthur Jensen, Ph.D. as an advocate of intelligence differences between "races" during the 70's; Nobel Prize winning physicist, William Shockley, advocating African sterilization in the 70's because of genetic inferiority; and Carlton Coon's publishing of *The Story of Man* in 1954, in which he said that the "major living races" had separate evolutionary histories. According to Coon, some races evolved into Homo Sapiens, or modern man, sooner than others. The European was of course the first to evolve and therefore more advanced. An example of this European consistency of psychosis that comes from the Maafa, that might surprise some people, is Charles Darwin.

Since Western culture holds Darwin in high esteem, most people are familiar with *On the Origins of Species*, published in 1859, while African people were still enslaved. However, most people are not told nor are they aware that the full title of the work is *On the Origin of Species by Means of Natural Selection, or The Preservation of Favoured Races in the Struggle for Life*. It is no mystery that *the* favored "race" from Darwin's perspective is the European. In *The Black Image in the White Mind*, George Frederickson relates:

> The contribution of Darwinism, therefore, is in its implication of cosmic advantages in the disappearance of "lower races" in the struggle for exitstence, was to make the prospect of Negro extinction under freedom more palatable than if it were considered an unavoidable tragedy, a regrettable necessity, or at best, a convenient solution to the American race problem. [14]

Serving as another example, the Maafa itself is probably the most profound indicator of a European exxagerated sense of superiority and the belittling of others. The arrogance of this inhumanity to fellow man and the horrendous treatment of Africans, allow Europeans to bear a resemblance to this personality disorder. Europeans also have traditionally failed to recognize their role in the degraded status of the masses of African people throughout the world, wherever Europeans have worked their psychotic ways. The parallels to the Paranoid personality disorder are endless.

The second personality definition that serves to help us establish a sense of European psychological damage tied with the Maafa is as follows:

Antisocial personalities (previously used designations: **psychopathic, sociopathic**) characteristically act out their con flicts and flout normal rules of social order. These persons are impulsive, irresponsible, amoral, and unable to forego immediate gratification. They cannot form sustained affectionate relation ships with others, but their charm and plausability may be highly developed and skillfully used for their own ends. They tolerate frustration poorly, and opposition is likely to illicit hostility, aggresion or serious violence. Their antisocial behavior shows little foresight and is not associated with remorse or guilt, since these people seem to have a keen capacity for rationalizing and for blaming their irresponsible behavior on others. Frustration and punishment rarely modify their behavior or improve their judge- ment and foresight. Owing to impulsivity, a person with an antiso cial personality may attempt suicide if his aggressions become turned inward instead of being directed against others. Dishon- esty manifested by lies, frequent geographic moves, and use of false identification are common. [15]

Again, in dealing with the historical and present deeds of Euro- pean people, the parallels to Antisocial personalities are numerous. A clear example of opposition eliciting European hostility, aggression *and* serious violence can be seen in the FBI's covert operations to destroy African organizations and leaders. From Dr. MartinLuther King and the NAACP to the Black Panthers and Malcolm X, the Counterintelligence Program, otherwise known as COINTELPRO, infiltrated, murdered and incited con- flict in African organizations dedicated to uplifting African people. Aside from the obvious damage that this caused in the hope that African people had for liberation and the fear it instilled, the negative propaganda aimed at African people that accompanied such European behaviors further con- tributed to damaging the psychological processes of Africans. This was especially true in the African conception of self and the validity of struggle.

The lack of remorse or guilt that accompanies the capacity for the Antisocial personality to rationalize and blame their irresponsibility on oth- ers, can be witnessed in two different extremes in the European cultural group. On the one hand, the United States and European nations have utilized African natural resources irresponsibly *and* criminally. And, as we addressed in the chapter entitled "Pawns in Population Politics," Euro- peans in the United States and in Europe have rationalized and blamed the results of this irresponsible use of resources on those who they victimized through the murder and brutality of colonization.

The other extreme can be see in groups like the Klan, Skinheads, Neo-Nazi's, etc. These groups have undergone a resurgence in popularity and exhibit pathologies of extremely violent behavior. Their lack of remorse or guilt when they kill individuals because they are African, gay, Jewish, etc., is rationalized by the Skinhead view, for example, that these groups are destroying the purity of the White race and undermining White Supremacy. Their pathology of violence has drawn media attention.

> Skinheads have murdered in every corner of the country. In New York in 1990, 29-year-old Julio Rivera was fatally stabbed and beaten with a hammer by three men connected with the Doc Martens Stompers because he was gay. Later that year in Houston, two skinheads conducted a "boot party" with a 15-year-old Vietnamese immigrant named Hung Truong. Just before he was stomped to death, according to a detective on the case, Truong pleaded, "Please stop. I'm sorry I ever came to your country. God forgive me." In Salem, Oregon, in September 1992, three members of the American Front group fire bombed the apartment of a black lesbian named Hattie Cohens and her roommate, a gay white man named Brian Mock, killing both. And a few months earlier in Birmingham, Alabama, three young skins awakened a homeless black man named Benny Rembert and knifed him to death.[16]

The activities of these types of groups are not limited to the United States. Wherever Europeans reside in contact with other cultural groups, there seems to be an element of the Antisocial personality.

The Compulsive personality also gives us a point of departure for examining European psychological scars.

> They pay attention to every detail and are therefore in danger of becoming entangled with means and forgetting the main purposes of their tasks. Compulsiveness is in tune with Western cultural standards, and when the disorder is not too marked, these people often are capable of high levels of achievement, especially in the sciences and other academic fields where order is desirable. On the other hand, they often feel a sense of isolation and have difficulties with interpersonal relationships in which their feelings are not under strict control, events are less predictable, and they must rely on others.[17]

Surprisingly, in the Compulsive personality description, the connection to "Western culture" is made for us. The Western compulsiveness, as well as such psychotic racism and advocacy of White World Supremacy as that of Darwin's natural selection and the Skinheads preserving of the White race, allows us to introduce Dr. Francis Cress Welsing's analysis of the psychology of Europeans.

Dr. Welsing's theories and analyses of European psychology are in depth. However, the brunt of her studies is evidenced in her functional definition of racism or white supremacy, from her work *The Isis Papers*.

> As a Black behavioral scientist and practicing general and child psychiatrist, my current functional definition of racism (white supremacy) is as follows: *the local and global power system structured and maintained by persons who classify themselves as white, whether consciously or subconsciously determined; this system consists of patterns of perception, logic, symbol formation, thought, speech, action and emotional response, as conduct simultaneously in all areas of people activity (economics, education, entertainment, labor, law, politics, religion, sex and war). The ultimate purpose of the system is to prevent white genetic annihilation on Earth -- a planet in which the overwhelming majority of people are classified as non-white (black, brown, red and yellow) by white-skinned people. All of the non-white people are genetically dominant (in terms of skin coloration) compared to the genetically recessive white-skinned people.* [18]

Another important contribution to an analysis of European thought is presented by Marimba Ani in *Yurugu: An African-Centered Critique of European Cultural Thought and Behavior.* Ani's exhaustive study examines European psychology, but approaches it from a cultural and behavioral perspective far too involved to encapsulize in a brief statement. However, we can gain some insight into Ani's conclusions through the following:

> What is it that the soul, mind, or pysche has that the body and senses do not? Clearly it is control and with control comes power as in "the ability to dominate." The desire (need) for control and power are the most important factors in understanding the European asili. [19]

Ani also gives an analysis, in *Yurugu*, of the European ideology of progress, which ties in to the Compulsive personality. As the Compulsive personality becomes overly concerned with the means and forgetting the purpose of tasks, Ani asserts that the European idea of progress "is concerned with the evolving, not with the end product." [20]

Normally when people have personality disorders they do not recognize that they are ill. This brings us to the point where we can ask about the diabolical nature of those who are aware that what they believe is a lie and what they do is wrong, but use lies and psychological manipulation to damage the minds of other people. The individuals who spread misinformation and cause psychological damage intentionally, fully aware of what they are doing, are different from those who are psychologically damaged. The agent of this psychosis is worse than those whose minds are poisoned to believe racist ideas and act upon them. The agent of psychosis caused all of the types of problems we have mentioned and was party to causing the suffering of the African ancestors during the Maafa. These same people see the suffering of people around the world today, have the power to affect change and do nothing to alleviate the problems. Instead, they may excacerbate human suffering for their own personal gain. This is a sickness of a different kind. This is evil and where identified should be met with unmerciful consequences.

****

Yes, there remain psychological scars from the Great Suffering and before there is any time to heal, new injuries form new scars in this world. The point of optimism is that when the body is injured the scar tissue is often tougher than the original tissue. African people have shown resilience by surviving the Great Suffering. Now, it is time for us to use the strength that we have gained from our injuries to help us return to sanity.

Dr. Richard King, in *African Origin of Biological Psychiatry*, talks about the collective unconscious memory recorded in all of our minds. It means that we possess all of the ancient African memories and experiences of our ancestors, we simply have to know how to access them. In fact, Dr. King says that we unconsciously receive these experiences from deeper levels of our mind. If this is true, then part of our psychological problem could be directly related to our internalization of foreign values and negative behaviors. These foreign values and negative behaviors are not only in conflict with our cultural/spiritual conception of rightness, but they are also causing internal, deep-mind level conflicts with the collective memories we possess from our African ancestors.

Fortunately, African people are on the road to recovery. We are begin to reclaim our African culture and minds. We are beginning to come to terms with our suffering and deal with it in a very healthy way. Consequently, we are moving closer to the balance and harmony that once made us a great people. Once we raise ourselves to a level of sanity, balance and harmony, it is then and only then that we will be able to return the world to a similar state of mind.

CHAPTER 12

THE AFRICAN CULTURAL AESTHETIC: RECLAIMING OURSELVES

The psychological experience of the Maafa has obviosly affected the standards we have for health and beauty. These standards or conceptions that we have of what is healthy and what is beautiful apply to mentality, physical appearance, art, music and literature. They are properly referred to as our aesthetic. The relationships we have to our aesthetic reflect deep seated, or subconscious attitudes. In other words, the rejection of self that is evident in African children who choose European dolls, while frowning upon African dolls, is an affirmation of a European aesthetic and an indication of self-hate. The child may not say, "I hate myself," but it is shown in the aesthetic that is rejected: the African one.

If African people do not have an African aesthetic to validify the beauty and value of themselves, this presents a problem. African people in this situation will adopt the aesthetic values of others. And, in as much as aesthetic values are standards, these people will aspire to the standards of others.

The problem is that an African can never be as European as a European, nor can an African be European at all for that matter, at least not in the sense that we use these terms. Consequently, the African as-pires to the unachievable, which is wholly achievable for the European for whom the standards are designed. The African then suffers from a sense of personal inadequacy and inferiority compared to the European who has achieved or at least come closer to the standard. Thus, whatever psycho-logical problems that made the African reject himself/herself to begin with are exacerbated.

Now this lies in the realm of psychology, but the importance of the African cultural aesthetic is in our psychological capacity to see our need to liberate ourselves from the cultural and psychological imposition of European people. With this realization, the recognition of a need for self-determination in all areas may follow. Can a person who does not value their own identity and aesthetic see the need for liberation in the truest sense manifested in self-determination, self-definition and self-sufficiency? It would seem that such a person could not see the need for true liberation.

The African who aspires towards a European aesthetic, for example, is aspiring toward a European mentality and physical appearance, as well as holding Europeans, their art, their music and their literature as the standard of beauty and value. This person becomes concerned with assimilation. Assimilation is the only way that this individual can achieve his or her aesthetic goals and have access to those things considered beautiful and valuable. Shelby Steele gives good examples of an assimilationist attitude coming from an African when he writes:

> There will be no end to despair and no lasting solution to any of our problems until we rely on individual effort within the American mainstream--rather than collective action against the mainstream--as our means of advancement. [1]

Even setting aside Steele's disturbing discouragement of collective action, it is obvious that this is an attitude that sees advancement as working with or assimilating into the "mainstream," which as a point of fact is synonymous with European culture and values. Within the context of subscribing to a European aesthetic, as the assimilationist must, it should not be a surprise that Mr. Steele's wife is European. This is not a statement on "interracial" relationships, but rather an observation that affirms and complements Mr. Steele's assimilationist attitude and consequent adoption of a European aesthetic.

To take this point a step further it is intersting to note that assimilation is defined as "The process whereby a minority group gradually adopts the customs and attitudes of the prevailing culture." [2] So, in fact, inherent in assimilation is the adoption of the European aesthetic.

At this point we can answer our initial question about the ability of a person who does not value their own cultural identity and aesthetic to be a participant in our struggle for liberation. The answer is that such an individual will not be able to struggle effectively for liberation. It would represent a contradiction, because they could not value European culture and its aesthetic, as well as fight meaningfully against its imposition on African people. Common sense and the definition of assimilation tell us that such a person seeks to have European culture imposed upon them, which means that they would not fight against this imposition for liberation.

The African cultural aesthetic and our embrace of it is extremely important to the movement towards African liberation. If a person and a collective group of people assign value and beauty to themselves and their creations, any repression of these things they hold valuable is unacceptable. Such repression is for all intents and purposes a repression of the people themselves. The natural reaction to this situation is to free oneself from this repression.

This is the way in which the celebration of our African cultural aesthetic is valuable to a healthy mind-state and our struggle for liberation. The importance of this celebration is incresed given the fact that the Maafa did much to destroy the African cultural aesthetic and push us towards the European aesthetic, while easily dehumanizing and oppressing us as a result. It would stand to reason that a reclamation of the African cultural aesthetic helps to reverse the harmful effects of the Maafa.

Maulana Karenga's writings about creative production in the African community are informative. His reference to the "Black aesthetic," in *Introduction to Black Studies*, was specifically related to "art," which he defined as creative production according to standards of beauty and relating to people's life experiences and aspirations. This is similar to our reference to the African cultural aesthetic, except that we include physical appearance and mentality with the art, music and literature of Karenga. Therefore, for our purposes the African cultural aesthetic is both creative production, as well as physical and mental standards of health and beauty that relate to a people's experiences and aspirations.

With this in mind, one meaning Karenga assigned to the "Black aesthetic" was "a criteria by which Black art could not only be judged in terms of its creativity and beauty, but also in terms of its social relevance." [3] If we place our definition of the African cultural aesthetic in place of "Black art," we can come away with the African cultural aesthetic as a definer of creativity and beauty, but more importantly as a socially relevant force, which substantiates what we have already mentioned about the role of this aesthetic in liberation.

With a clear idea of what the African cultural aesthetic means and a rather broad defintion of it, the question might be raised as to exactly what the African cultural aesthetic is. How does one identify it and what are the parameters that are used to define beauty? The answer to the question is whatever African people as a collective and as individuals find beautiful and valuable, from a perspective of sanity and cultural grounding. In other words, anything that African people produce and all the ways in which African people appear and think are beautiful and valued. The perspective of sanity and cultural grounding simply means that creations and mentalities of African people that are a result of self-hate, miseducation, acceptance of the European aesthetic, brainwashing, etc., are not accepted as part of the African cultural aesthetic. It is important to keep three things in mind when we refer to the African cultural aesthetic.

1) It does not bind individuals to a homogenous acceptance of what beauty and health is. It merely establishes a sane, collective and self-affirming framework in which people decide what their own personal preferences are. The African cultural aesthetic validifies the African self, which the Maafa has done so much to destroy. Put simply, within the African cultural aesthetic people may be themselves and find value and beauty in being themselves.

2) There is no list of attributes that a person must adhere to in order to be African. There is also no line one crosses that says they now accept the African cultural aesthetic.

3) The African cultural aesthetic, because of the value assigned to the African self, means that fighting for liberation from repression of this aesthetic is a must. Repression of the aesthetic means repression of the people who accept the aesthetic.

In reclaiming the African cultural aesthetic, the process is almost as important as the end product of reclamation. While accepting the African cultural aesthetic will mean fighting for liberation when it is repressed, the regaining of a knowledge of self which is part of reclaiming the aesthetic is empowering in itself.

Because of the Maafa, the masses of African people are in the unfortunate position of having to rediscover who they are and from where they have come. Therefore, accepting the African cultural aesthetic usually necessitates this rediscovery. We find out who we are and from where we have come through studying all that has been withheld from us about ourselves. The more one studies and understands his or her history, origins and orientation in the world, the more beautiful things that are African become. There is a natural progression towards further and further acceptance of the aesthetic.

The type of material studied in this reclamation process includes history and current events, which in themselves serve as a spring board for recognition of the need for the liberation of African people. It is somewhat of an awakening to see the injustice and horror of the Maafa, the suffering of African people for hundreds of years up to the present, the misuse of information and miseducation of the masses and the imposition of European psychotic behaviors and culture on the world's people with all of its destructive effects.

Study, in and of itself, can lead to a reclamation of the African cultural aesthetic and the development of a conscious participant in the struggles of African people. This can take place when a person's only objective is to acquire a little extra knowledge, with no notions of liberation or the African cultural aesthetic. That is the power of knowledge.

So, reclaiming ourselves is a necessity, but there is much work to do. Currently, African people have many problems accepting themselves as they are. Many of us have notions of what "good hair" is and what "bad hair" is. Almost invariably, good hair means hair that is straight, less coarse, soft and curly, etc. Bad hair tends to be defined as the type of hair that is natural to many African people, which is coarse, curly, and so on. The European aesthetic has dictated that to solve this hair problem, African people must aspire to hair that looks like that which is more common in European people. As a result, jheri curls, conks, weaves, Bone Strait hair relaxer, perms and any number of other mechanisms for aspiring to a European aesthetic have developed in the African community. At the same time, people with natural hair styles have been shunned as having bad hair, naps, cockleburs, looking like buckwheat (African locks) and any number of other insults and jests.

Fortunately, we are entering a time in 1995 where natural styles are becoming more and more popular. Braids, locks, short natural cuts and afros are more often seen. However, the problem of hair still exists. What the African cultural aesthetic does is validify that natural African hair styles are all beautiful, from straight to curly and from soft to coarse. The many different hair textures of African people hold their own beauty. There is no such thing as good hair and bad hair. There may be well groomed hair versus unkept hair, but not good and bad hair. This enables people to work with what the creator has given them. If one likes long hair that flows, grow locks. African locks, commonly known as dreadlocks, are the most healthy way to grow the texture of hair that many African people have. It will grow much longer than permed hair and looks much better than weaves. There is also no limit to the styles that mature locks can be worn in. Well groomed locks are one of the most beautiful hair-styles there are. If one likes low maintenance hair, a short natural cut is good for both men and women. The list goes on. The point is that African people need not aspire to a hair style that is in conflict with their natural hair and the African cultural aesthetic. European hair texture and style, or the emulation of it, is not *the* standard.

Although a seemingly trivial thing, comfort with one's hair is a component of being comfortable with one's self. Comfort with self is a healthy state of mind. When self is valued, any repression of it is met with a struggle for liberation. That is where we find ourselves in the aftermath of the Maafa; we need to becomfortable enough and knowledgeable enough about who we are to recognize that there is a struggle to be waged for the liberation of African people.

Another issue often raised is with regard to skin color. It is enough that we have been mistreated by Europeans on the basis of our pigmentation, but we have also mistreated one another. Both extremes, very light skin and very dark skin, have been maligned *and* falsely celebrated by African people. African people with very light skin have been teased, considered "not really black," called half breeds and high yellow. At the same time, some light skinned Africans have received privileges because of their light skin, looked down on dark skin, been valued as better looking because of their light skin, etc. On the other hand, dark skinned Africans have been called tar babies, spooks, been teased and mistreated. At the same time, some dark skinned Africans have looked down on light skin, considered themselves "real" Africans, and thought they were more down with the struggle because of their dark skin.

First, there are any number of brown, black, yellow and reddish hues of African people. The presence of some degree of pigmentation is only one dimension of being African. Realizing that very few of us, if any in the Western hemisphere, are *purely* of African ancestry, African comes to represent the culture and values we identify with, as well as the presence of pigmentation.

Secondly, the African cultural aesthetic affirms that every shade of black, brown, red and yellow that African people are born with is beautiful. In fact, one aspect of the beauty of African people is the diversity of skin color that we have, while remaining African. This helps to bring us all together regardless of skin color and assure that we fight the oppression that makes us all suffer because we have pigmentation period.

Another aesthetic issue that we have had to deal with is that part of the Maafa's legacy was to buffoon and animalize the physical characteristics of African people. To this day many Africans are ashamed of their broad noses or their full lips. African people make fun of one another based on these characteristics. Many African men seek the European aesthetic when they are looking for African women with thin noses and small lips. This is not to say that some African people don't have such characteristics naturally, it is simply a comment on the men who seek them for the wrong reasons. Some of these same African men and boys choose European women to be their mates because they have accepted the European aesthetic.

The African cultural aesthetic remedies this situation, because African features are beautiful and valued in this aesthetic. Full lips and broad noses are beautifully African, as is whatever features one is born with. This is pride. It nullifies the need for the nose jobs that plague African celebrities. It wipes out the madness that says you must have European features to be beautiful.

The African aesthetic is also important in the areas of art, music and literature. Art is a broad term and applies to our creative production from painting to movie production. The African cultural aesthetic dictates that our stories and images are beautiful and can be presented as such in our art. Whether it be the depiction of lovers on canvas or in movies, our lives are beautiful and we are beautiful. We are far too majestic a people to be pigeon holed into such things as movies about drug dealers and tragedy. Our stories of love are not profane, nor are they vulgar. African kisses, hand holding, walks in the park, love making and family gatherings are beautiful to see on the screen. The African cultural aesthetic says that our young African filmmakers can make socially responsible stories about African life and they will be beautiful works of art.

As another art form our music has always contained messages and our aesthetic allows our musical artists to aspire to the highest level of beauty in the expression of life. It needn't be about betraying the craft for a few dollars. Speaking truth through music has the highest value in our aesthetic. Communicating with one another has value. From the sacred drums of Africa to the conscious music of today, music with a message is beautiful and music that simply moves the soul is beautiful.

Our literature can reflect us also. African people need to leave records of where we are, where we have been and where we are going. The word is a strong way to do this. Our stories must be told. Whether we write poetry, non-fiction, fiction or put on the robes of a griot, our stories are the standards according to our aesthetic. And, our love, losses, triumphs, tragedies, families, struggles, laughing and crying are all valued.

African is beautiful. When African becomes beautiful the repression of things African is ugly and the African essence is valued too much not to be fought for. The African cultural aesthetic validifies our beauty as a people. It is to this we should aspire.

153

Chapter 13

RAISE THE FLAG, WAVE THE COLORS

As African people continue to move beyond the Great Suffering, thought needs to be given to our seriousness about liberation. The issue of nation building has been examined from the broad perspective of possibilities and objectives relating to institution building, as well as self-determination. This certainly requires serious African people working together, but within what framework can this be achieved? In other words, what will be the catalyst for the endeavor of African people building institutions collectively for the purpose of benefitting Africans worldwide?

It seems that there must be a common bond, that extends beyond and springboards off of our realization of African global connections. The need for there to be a "vehicle" for the movement and activities of African people seems apparent. Even this need seems to be two fold. Mentally, we need an identification with one another on a global scale. The Maafa, and a proper understanding of it, can be that mental rallying point and "vehicle." Physically, we need something concrete to rally around. Africa is concrete as a continent, but to most Africans in the diaspora only in the sense of abstract ancestral connections, unity and culture. It is a continent, not a "vehicle" for our movement on a mass level.

The question then becomes, what do we mean by a physical or concrete vehicle for our mass movement? Some insight can be gained by looking at other cultural groups that have achieved some sense of self determination, with whom African people constantly are compared to and compare themselves to.

European Jewish people have been an example of a people who have built there own institutions and controlled there own destiny. Consequently, they are a powerful player in politics and are the sole dictators of how European Jewish issues, culture and people will be defined and addressed. How is the Jewish community, who have certainly suffered persecution, different from the African community? Aside from the differences in our historical experiences, the Jewish community has one very important thing that African people in the diaspora do not. They have a nation, with sovereignty, defined borders, a military and a flag: Israel.

The argument can be made that African people in the diaspora have a homeland, which is Africa. However, key differences are that Africa is a continent and not a nation, our connection to Africa is more cultural and less politically empowered, and even the African nations that we might identify with have the same problems of European domination that we have in the diaspora. Africa is a valued part of our identity, but neither continent nor its countries are in any position to defend and define the African global community as Israel does for Jewish people.

The same observations can be made regarding Asians who come to the U.S. Asians certainly don't share the same type of historical oppression and suffering as African people, but in their status as a people of color in a European dominated society they have nations to return to. Koreans may return to Korea or bring family from Korea, as is the case for other Asian cultural groups. To this advantage of nationalism, add the psychological advantage that comes from having a nation and a flag to identify with.

The best example might be a look at the emotional impact that the American flag has on some, as it blows in the wind while the Star Spangled banner is sung. This tends to be especially heightened for some people with the pride of emotional rallying events like the Olympics. For African people, the American flag blowing in the wind and the words of the anthem, speaking of "the land of the free and the home of the brave," represents a supreme contradiction. Africans who are conscious and awake often times cease to draw anything positive from this nationalist activity. Africans who are still moved by it often retain an irrational loyality to America's rhetoric, which operates against their abilility to be self-determined and benefit from nationalism in the way that Jewish people do with Israel.

So, it would seem clear that African people need something in addition to the mental vehicle of the Maafa, the abstract (but positive) cultural identification with Africa, and the global unity based on common history, culture and experience. Perhaps nation building should have some implicit plans for a sovereign nation? This would not mean that all African people from the diaspora would live in such a nation, just as all Jewish people do not live in Israel. It simply means that there would be a homeland open to all African people on the continent and in the diaspora for citizenship, which offers Africans a base of world political, economic, cultural and military support.

There are positives and negatives to this proposition. On the negative side, where would a sovereign nation be established. African people should not wish to replicate the Jewish establishment of Israel by waging war on people who might occupy the land that we want, nor would we be able to do so lacking the Western military support that Israel received. Also, African people should not be arrogant enough to presume to relocate in an existing African country and take it over. Problems with that particular plan would be conflict with our own African brothers and sisters, as well as stepping into a situation where Europeans already have a foothold through colonization.

On the positive side, perhaps there would be the possibility of a block of African countries selling portions of each of their nations for the establishment of a new African nation. Europeans shouldn't be involved because their historical record and current deeds make it foolish to trust them, their cultural values are not appropriate and African people need to do for self. It would be upon Africans to raise the flag and wave the colors of our own sovereign nation. This would give African people the ability to start fresh and free of damaging European influence. There are already many African people worldwide with the skills, consciousness and will to begin such an endeavor.

If we were to actually begin planning for such a nation, how would we do it? The first step might be establishing the philosophical and ideological framework in which the building of this nation would take place. This includes the reasons for building a nation, the values of such a nation and the role that such a nation would play in the lives of African people worldwide. For the most part, all the elements of such a framework have been laid, not only in this book, but in the works and deeds of numerous Pan-Africanists, nationalists and activists in the liberation struggle of African people. This philosophical and ideological framework would also determine the types of individuals who would participate in this task.

Next, those brothers and sisters who would begin the ground work of nation building might organize in a fashion that would allow for ideas to be converted into action plans. Much like the numerous summits that African people have on a variety of issues, those with like minds and consciousness could get together to work out the "how to" aspects of building this nation. An essential component of this would be conducting the initial talks and negotiating with the African countries who would provide land. From such a summit, a contingent of planners would need to be funded for full time work on the implementation of the plans.

Planners groups might be broken into categories such as Nation Negotiation and Legal Team; Agriculture, Ecology and Environment; Government, Foreign Affairs and Economy; Education, Social Values and Culture; Technology and Science; Health and Medicine; Communications and Media; Transportation; Water Treatment and Waste Management;

Architecture, Construction, Surveying and Development; National Image; and Military Operations, Procedures and Ethics to name a few.

The responsibilities of the Nation Negotiation and Legal Team might include the continued contact with African nations donating land, monitering of all legal issues surrounding nation building efforts and serving as diplomats between the proposed African nation and the world. The Nation Negotiation and Legal Team would also serve as a body that the other planning groups could consult for the feasbility of certain plans.

The Agriculture, Ecology and Environment planning group would be responsible for studying the land set aside for the new nation and advising other planning groups on how their activities will impact the environment, as well as the balance between nature and humans. An important interaction of this group might be with the Health and Medicine planning group. There might be a need to assess health issues involved in the adaptation of those Africans coming from the diaspora to their new environment in Africa. Such issues as susceptability to unfamiliar diseases and environemtal conditions could be worked out.

The Government, Foreign Affairs and Economy planning group would come together to produce a model constitution, governmental infrastructure, government policies, legal structures, national budgetary considerations and the nature of involvement with other countries. This group would probably work most closely with the Nation Negotiation and Legal Team.

The all important task of determining how to shape the minds of the nation would fall into the hands of the Education, Social Values and Culture planning group. The administration and content of the nation's schools would be mapped out by this planning group. Philisophical and ideological issues concerning the purpose of education would also be articulated. (Issues such as those in Chapter 6. See Chancellor Williams) Additional responsibilities of this group would include the types of social values and culture to be articulated to the masses in education. The cultural aspect of this group's activities would necessarily include study of the languages and traditions of the African populations that border the proposed national territory. It would also include decisions as to the primary language to be spoken in the dealings of the nation. Swahili is a possibility, as was mentioned in Chapter 6. There would be a definite need for interaction between this group and all of the others, to ensure consistency of purpose and direction for the nation.

The Technology and Science group would be responsible for socially and environmentally responsible, cutting edge technology to benefit the nation. This group would ensure that technology is utilized well, but does not usurp civilization. Progress for the sake of progress and science without ethics would not be tolerated.

Maintaining the good health of the nation's population would naturally fall under the auspices of the Health and Medicine planning group. In conjunction with the Architecture, Construction, Surveying and Development group, hospitals and health care fascilities would be built to best suit health care provisions.

The Communications and Media planning group would provide for the means of information flow in the nation. Wire services, telecommunications, fiber optic technology and all of the other intricacies of communication would be worked out by this group. A synergistic relationship between the Communications and Media group and the Technology and Science group would be necessary for communications satellite technology, among other types of high tech communication.

The roles of the Transportation planning group would be mapping out efficient routes and means of transportation for the new nation. Cooperation with the Agriculture, Ecology and Environment planning group would be necessary.

For the safety and health of the African nation's population, the Water Treatment and Waste Management group would play a key role. They would organize the building of water treatment fascilities and the management of all forms of waste.

Aesthetically, environmentally and structurally, the African nation would benefit from the planning of the Architecture, Construction, Surveying and Development group. This planning body would organize the initial layout of the government, hospital, education and other structures to be established. They would also team with the Agriculture, Ecology and Environment group to do things such as establish zones in which the natural environment will be preserved, places where certain types of buildings and businesses would be harmful to nature, etc.

The Military Operations, Procedures and Ethics planning group would be responsible for the organization of a disciplined, high tech, educated and responsible military force. As much as is possible for a group of men and women trained to execute destructive force, this military would be spiritually minded, culturally grounded, humanitarian and intelligent. Unnecessary barbarism and immorality would be avoided to the fullest extent, realizing that war often renders those who fight it insane. Also, the posture of the military would be to protect African lives and well being, with no emphasis on expanionist military aggression.

Finally, the National Image planning group would feel the pulse of African people to come up with such things as appropriate anthems, symbolic representations and outward projections of the new nation. This group would also work with African people to choose a name for the new

African nation and provide for a flag to raise and colors to wave.

Such an idea for the founding of a new African nation is worthy of *consideration* at the least. It represents an opportunity for a new beginning for African people worldwide in terms of a power base, politcally and economically. The ability to start from scratch, benefiting from our collective knowledge and history of struggle, is attractive. It would also mean the opportunity to create an environment free of today's corruptive, deep rooted, insane mindstates found in many European communities and institutions. Only those African people who wanted to relocate to this new nation would do so, but all African people could benefit from its establishment, whether they be Africans from the continent or in the diaspora. The new African nation would become the physical "vehicle" for the movement toward self-determination and worldwide liberation for African people. It would be the validation of our struggle, the embodiment of our potential, the support for our activities and our release from dependency. Existing African nations could both benefit from its strengths and contribute to its development as the representative of the African struggle. This new nation could even be the crossroads of African unity throughout the continent, spurring the development of the Federated States of Africa spoken of in Chapter 6.

Considering our circumstances as a people who have come through the Great Suffering and continue to suffer for it, is this new African nation a possibility? Will we ever raise the flag and wave the colors of our own sovereign nation? Of course, long years would be spent in the proper planning by the various planning groups before a corps of engineers would be sent to be the first settlers. One can only imagine the awesome feelings of pride and accomplishment that would result from seeing the first engineering corps of brothers and sisters from all over the Western hemishphere leaving for the "promised land" to meet Africans on the continent and began building this new reality. Can the masses of African people even begin to conceive of such a reality?

` If African people are unable to even conceive the possibility of building a new nation, how serious are we about liberation? Throughout history, when people have been oppressed without relief, they have built new nations to uphold the values that they were deprived of where they resided. The poor amongst the English masses where oppressed and certain religions persecuted, catalyzing the birth of the United States. The European Jews were persecuted and murdered in their Holocaust, furthering the movement towards the birth of Israel and fulfilling what European Jews considered Biblical Prophesy, by the return to their Biblical Holy Land .

What is the mind-state of African people, who live in exile from the continent of Africa having suffered through the Maafa, if they cannot even *conceive* of building a new nation? Perhaps if we are at the very least able to conceive of such a reality, all of our activities towards building educational, economic, social and cultural institutions where we currently live will be fruitful. The level of seriousness that we have about liberation is an indication to our seriousness as a people. A people seriously about freedom can conceive of dying for it, so what are we if we can't even imagine a nation of our own?

These are serious questions because the circumstances of the African existence are serious. One does not have to want to leave America to be serious. There are plenty of brothers and sisters who make significant contributions to the struggle for African liberation and do not wish to leave the home they have made in the Western hemisphere. However, even these brothers and sisters should be able to contemplate the possibility of a new nation, even if their contemplation finds serious flaws with the concept. To deny the thought out of hand with no good reason, is a statement on our silliness and naivité.

All is not lost, however, if we do not find it feasible or possible to build our own nation. We still have options to exercise to prevent us from going down in history as the silliest of our people to ever walk the face of the earth. We can decide to raise the flag and wave the colors right where we are in North America, South America, the Carribean, Africa, Central America, Europe and elsewhere. African people can still fulfill the promise of nation building and controlling their own destinies. A nation can exist without the boundaries of sovereignty if the people who comprise it are unified and committed to one another and the struggle. If those people control their means of survival and come to the table as equals with other people, not begging for anything, then that is a nation of people. Then, if we do not have the flag of a new African nation to wave, we can raise our forever meaningful flag and wave the colors of the red, the black and the green.

CHAPTER 14

THE ANCIENT AFRICAN MODEL

There is nothing to say that with the advance of time, there comes inevitable progress. As we look at the state of today's world and the predicament of the United States in particular, it is not difficult to see the corruption, crime, murder, brutality, environmental destruction, oppression and theft that occur at the highest levels of society, not to mention the depths at which the masses of all people are languishing. The advances of today's technology have not been accompanied by an improvement in the overall human condition.

Civilization is defined as "An advanced state of intellectual, cultural, and material development in human society, marked by progress in the arts and sciences, the extensive use of writing, and the appearance of complex political and social institutions." [1]

Given this definition of civilization, can we automatically make the assumption that where we are today, as a result of the advance of time, can be considered progress as compared to any other time in history? Certainly, today's world is technologically advanced, but even the degree of progress made in technology is to be questioned, as we shall see.

Coming out of the Maafa these questions are important because as we look for paradigms and models of what we want to achieve as African people, we should be striving towards the best models and incorporate the good from all models. The question then is where do we look for a model? Do we look at today's world powers and the people who are currently dominating the masses, or is there something else? Chancellor Williams wrote that:

> Western society has failed and is unable to cope with its
> internal social problems or its international crises precisely because
> both Western religion and Western education have failed. And they
> have failed, we insist, because they have rushed ahead expanding the
> shadow of civilization and unwittingly leaving civilization behind--
> "civilization itself" being a society primarily concerned with the

163

improvement of *man*, not just things; *improvement of man*, not just his environment and creature comforts. A higher standard of living should mean *a higher standard of man.* [2]

Given this assessment, it is clear that if we are to look for a model of nation building, human upliftment and civilization, our current society is not it. If we believe, as Chiekh Anta Diop did, that "Those who cannot serve us as examples, are not qualified to offer us advice, much less give us orders," [3] then we will break from this Western paradigm or model that many of us try to emulate.

Perhaps a most helpful option, at this time and in our circumstances, is to turn our eyes and minds toward the ancient African model. What we mean by ancient African model, is in fact a look at an amalgamation of ancient historical African paradigms in the form of such societies as Kemet (Egypt), Nubia (Kush or Ethiopia) and even such societies as the Dogon, Mali, Songhay and Ghana, (even though they may not be considered ancient). In fact, the Dogon still exist in West Africa.

There is a unity of African culture, with its diverse manifestations. So, adopting from many societies is more than appropriate to achieve our goal. This is important, not only because these African societies have more to offer us in terms of a model of civilization, but they also represent our historical and cultural consciousness being restored as we study them.

Rather than doing a historical overview of each of these African societies, we can look briefly at some of the vital areas in which they can inform us. Because life's institutions in most of these African frameworks were inseparable from one another it would be rather difficult to break our discussion into concise categories such as education, science, religion, etc. All of these elements exist in abundance in the African societies we will look at; however, not as separate from one another as we are accustomed to in current Western paradigms.

Before we begin, it is also important to note that this is not to advocate a complete return to any single ancient way of life. Realistically, this examination is for the purpose of adapting the best our history has to offer to our present circumstances.

There is perhaps no more glorious and awe inspiring an ancient culture as that of those Africans of the Nile: Kemet. Given the wondrous accomplishments of these ancient African people, it would be instructive to look at their educational process. However, two factors limit our ability to learn more about education in Kemet. First, there is this fact that Asa Hilliard, a prominent African scholar and educator, illuminated.

We are hampered in our attempt to learn about ancient

Egyptian education not only by widespread loss of documentary materials, by the destruction of social institutions and civilizations, including their library records, and by years of prejudice and neglect; but we are also hindered by the fact that some of the most important parts of the educational process were conducted in "secret." Much of the tradition was passed on orally to the prepared initiate. [4]

The second limiting factor is that it is nearly impossible to talk about education in Kemet without discussing religion, Medu Netcher or MDU NTR (hieroglyphics), philosophy and other aspects of daily life. Typical of African cultures, Kemet saw the world very holistically with no clear cut lines and no absolutes. The complexity and beauty of Kemet's philosophy and holistic worldview is still baffling and at a level superior to what we have been able to achieve today. However, despite these difficulties, we will proceed.

Where the West has failed in the purpose of education, Kemet was successful in producing more complex citizens. Part of this is due to the expressly spiritual focus of education and the inseparability of education from general life. This unity of all things is illustrated in the fact that the foremost educational institutions in Kemet are recognized to have been the Mystery Schools. These institutions educated priests through initiations that occurred over many, many years and took them from their lower self, or material presence, to their higher self, or moral and spiritual connection to their NTR or god-force within. This represented the highest learning in the society. Initiates would ascend to a point where they transcended bodily fetters, attained inner sight or use of the Third Eye, and achieved a state called "geru ma," the achievement of the balance and order of one's being and control of thought, instinct and emotion.

The specific relevance of Mystery Schools to education, in our segmented modern sense, is in the fact that the Mysteries were representative of more than the spiritual ascendence to higher levels. Part of reaching those higher levels included educational principles. Part of the Mystery School curriculum consisted of the Seven Liberal Arts which are grammar, arithmetic, rhetoric, dialectic, geometry, astronomy, and music. [5] Other principles of instruction involved the ten virtues described by George G. M. James in *Stolen Legacy*, which follow, as related by Asa Hilliard in *Kemet and the African Worldview*.

1. Control of thought
2. Control of action
3. Devotion of purpose
4. Faith in the Masters ability to teach the truth

5. Faith in ones ability to assimilate the truth
6. Faith in ourself to wield the truth
7. Freedom of resentment under persecution
8. Freedom of resentment under wrong
9. Ability to distinguish right from wrong
10. Ability to distinguish the real from unreal [6]

These were just the basic foundations of knowledge to these ancient ancestors. These were the tasks of the neophyte. These virtues were achieved by and applied to the participation, observation, and study of nature. This study was a never ending process carrying one to the point of harmony with the earth and the heavens. Initiates progressed to higher levels of scholarship which included specializing or seeking the "Holy Orders." George G. M. James described this specialization:

> (a) The Singer or Odus, who must know two books of Hermes dealing with Music i.e., the hymns of the Gods.
> (b) The Horoscopus, who must know the four books of Hermes dealing with Astronomy.
> (c) The Hierogrammat, who must know the hieroglyphics, cosmography, geography, astronomy and the topography of Egypt and Land Surveying.
> (d) The Stolistes, who must know the books of Hermes that deal with slaughter of animals and the process of embalming.
> (e) The Prophetes, who is the President of the temple, and must know ten books of Hermes dealing with higher esoteric theology and the whole education of priests.
> (f) The Pastophori, who must know six books of Hermes which are medical books, dealing with physiology, the diseases of male and female, anatomy, drugs and instruments. [7]

James goes on to describe the sciences that dealt with the monuments and the architecture, engineering, masonry and everything involved in the erection of some of the most awe inspiring, glorious, scientifically precise structures in the history of the world. There was also the description of the secret sciences which included symbolism and sacred magic.

Most people are familiar with the hieroglyphics of Kemet, which are properly referred to as MDU NTR (Medu Netcher). This was the sacred writing and language of James' *Hierogrammat*. The study of MDU NTR is itself an educational experience. Anyone who has studied or studies this sacred writing is aware of its challenging complexity in terms of grammatical structure that makes English seem like a simple language. Also, the meaning of MDU NTR exceeds the mere expression and description of the physical world. MDU NTR is rich and multi-dimensional, employing symbols, written characters, colors, and the arrangement or order of all of these elements to produce esoteric expression and spiritual power.

All that has been described was education in the truest sense of the word and it met the requirements of Chancellor Williams from the beginning of this chapter; education for the improvement of man. In the description James gave of the "Holy Orders" he was addressing the *42 Books of Hermes* and the sciences contained within them. Hermes was in fact the Greek name for Djehuti, also known by the Greek name Thoth. Djehuti is the divine scribe/creator of science/creator of medicine/articulator of speech, represented most often by the human body with an Ibis head and the scribe's utensils in his hands.

This brings us to a relevant statement concerning the vast influence of education in Kemet. The Greeks had names for all of the Netchers or divine essences of God found in Kemet. Most significantly, Greek philosophers regularly traveled to Kemet to become the neophytes of the priests and would study for decades. This includes one of the West's most valued classical theorists, Plato.

All of this education, and all of life, for the ancients was encompassed by and obligated to follow what is known as Maat. Maat is a powerful framework or philosophy of life that accompanies all activities and relationships. The Seven Virtues of Maat are Truth, Justice, Reciprocity, Order, Balance, Harmony, and Compassion. Individuals are supposed to speak Maat and do or practice Maat. Another component of Maat is encompassed in the *42 Declarations of Innocence* which espouse all of the elements one sees in the *Ten Commandments*, and a great deal more. The difference is that the *42 Declarations of Innocence* were not "commandments" enforced from on high, but declarations of right thought and action by the Maatian. Also, besides the fact that there were 42 declarations and only ten commandments, the *42 Declarations of Innocence* appeared thousands of years before the *Ten Commandments*.

Thus, it is easy to see that the highest education of ancient Kemet went far beyond the regurgitation of information or the compartmentalization of knowledge. It went far beyond the West's belief in absolute and objective ideas, separate from bias, emotion, spirituality, all of which are inferior in the eyes of Western educational philosophy. And, the fruits of Western education, at least 5,000 years after the Golden Age of Kemet, cannot compare with nor understand the fruits of ancient Kemet.

Another way in which we can assess the education in Kemet is by looking at the fruits of it that still baffle modern scholars. The evidence of vast skills and advanced knowledge they left behind reflect nothing less than a highly advanced and complete educational system. There are no pictures that can match the awesome majesty of being in Kemet and witnessing the splendor of what is left behind after thousands of years. Everyone knows of the pyramids, but perhaps do not know of their true beauty. The true beauty of the Great Pyramid is described well by Anthony Browder in *Nile Valley Contributions To Civilization.*

> Today, the basis of geography is the system of latitude and longitude used to measure the surface of our planet and to chart its surface with supreme accuracy. Most people think of this as an invention of the modern world because it requires a working knowledge of a higher form of mathematics such as spherical trigonometry. However, we find this exact knowledge incorporated into the interior and exterior measurements of the Great Pyramid.
>
> The pyramids perimeter (the sum of its base lengths) is 3,023 feet, which is precisely equal to one-half minute of a degree of latitude at the equator, or one forty-three thousand two hundredth (1:43,200) of the polar circumference of the Earth. [8]

Browder eloquently explains further measurements of the Great Pyramid and their direct relationship to the precise dimensions of the Earth. Such measurements are capable today only with the use of the highest technology of satellites and similar high tech devices. Mr. Browder also describes the immense proportions, in terms of the size of the Great Pyramid, that accompany its technological and scientific precision.

In the city now called Luxor in modern day Kemet (Waset to the ancient people of Kemet) the incredible ruins of two grand temples remain. Much of the education that we have described probably took place in these types of temples. The temples are the Ipet-Isut (Temple of Karnak) and the Shemayit-Ipet (Temple of Luxor). These centers of education, as well as religion or spirituality, are themselves scientific marvels of architectural brilliance.

Further to the South of Kemet in Abu Simbel, the Funerary of Rameses is a breath taking giant of a structure with the aesthetic beauty of African features and images chiseled into the side of a mountain, and the scientific, architectural and spiritual precision typical of Kemet. A single example of the scientific superiority of Kemet, seen in this funerary, is the amazing qualities of the Holy of Holies. The Holy of Holies is the deepest and smallest chamber in the funerary, which contains an alter and was the place where only the priest and King Rameses himself were permitted to enter. The walls of this chamber were coated in gold and there was an altar in the center of the room.

Now, the truly astounding spiritual and scientific fact is that this huge funerary was so precisely aligned architecturally that on two days of the year a single shaft of light would illuminate the Holy of Holies for a few exact moments. Those two days were the coronation date of Rameses and his birthdate, obviously days that were specific and not by chance. This illumination was made all the more glorious by the effect of the gold laden walls of the Holy of Holies reflecting the sunlight. Far from just a pretty site, this required such a vast knowledge of science and architecture that when the West tampered with the position of the temple on the mountainside, they were unable to reproduce the effect, even with the vast knowledge of modern science.

In terms of the spiritual significance of this illumination, it must be remembered that the sun is the symbol of Ra or God. It is the life giver, as is seen in inscriptions that show ankhs, symbols of life, on the ends of the suns rays as they come down to earth. Therefore, on the two days of illumination there was a communion with God in the Holy of Holies, in the form of the sun's rays.

In terms of medicine, specific temples were also dedicated to healing and the medical arts such as Kom Ombo. On the walls of Kom Ombo, medical instruments such as scalpels, clamps, surgical saws, pharmacist's mortar and pestle, and numerous other instruments are inscribed in the walls in the clearest detail. Medical documents such as the *Edwin Smith* and *Ebers* papyri contain descriptions of medical diagnoses, case studies, surgical procedures and medical terms for all parts of the brain, nervous system and anatomy in general. (Works like Anthony Browder's *Nile Valley Contributions to Civilization*, Ivan Van Sertima's *Egypt Revisited* and *Blacks in Science*, Richard King's *African Origin of Biological Psychiatry*, Charles Finch's *Echoes of the Old Darkland*, Yosef ben Jochanaan's *Abu Simbel to Giza*, and numerous others describe the unimaginable sophistication of the ancient civilization of Kemet in a depth that cannot even be approached in this work.)

The holistic package we have examined of moral, spiritual and scientific advancement is unarguably beyond what our current society will ever reach, and is obviously indicative of an educational infrastructure that supported and perpetuated it. These are the types of models we should look to for our own development. Approaching Maat is one way in which many Africans today are uplifting themselves through the inspiration of the ancestors.

Kemet is truly a splendor, especially in all that remains as evidence of its greatness, but by no means is it the only African model. The Dogon of West Africa are contemporary Africans maintaining the old traditions and baffling modern science. Once again, in the Dogon you have an education that is inseparable from spirituality, religion, nature and all other aspects of life.

The Dogon of Mali have a body of knowledge concerning the heliacal rising of a star in the Sirius Star System, which plays a role in the education of the Hogons (priests) and the religion of the Dogon. In the startling knowledge the Dogon have of "po tolo" or Sirius B, a star invisible to the naked eye, we see again the connections already mentioned between education, science, philosophy and religion.

The Dogon have tracked the orbit of Sirius B to an accuracy that rivals modern scientific astronomical observation capabilities. Their knowledge of this invisible star is all the more astonishing since their age old religion is grounded in this knowledge, making their observations far more advanced than the West's recent scientific accomplishments. They also know of the densities of stars and their brightness, among other qualities, all without the use of high powered telescopes or satellites.

The holistic nature of African knowledge construction, seen with the Dogon and the people of Kemet, notes the fact that there is a way of knowing beyond current Western standards of abstract, objective, emotionless, aspiritual science. In fact, the way in which African historical accomplishments continue to amaze and perplex modern scientists gives African knowledge construction a more than valid position in the world. This can be a point of departure for the children of the Maafa to assign the utmost importance and pride to who and what we are. We are the descendants of these ancient people of genius and spirit. Our potential is recorded in their historical accomplishments.

The Dogon process of education through initiation to different levels, involving years of study, is similar to that of Kemet. The French anthropologists who lived and studied with the Dogon for 25 years learned a great deal about this educational process. Hunter Adams III describes their experience as follows:

> At first they received the "word at face value" (simple knowledge), then the "word on the side," then the "word from behind." Only in 1947--16 years later--had the elders decided that they were ready to receive the "clear word," the abstract and esoteric knowledge. Now they could learn the Dogon's most sacred knowledge--the realization of the nature of creation, from the creation of the stars and spiraling galaxies to the creation of plants--and to know the purpose of human experience. Yet in the end, although privy to an extremely secret body of knowledge, Griaule and Dieterlen still had reached only

the "slight acquaintance" level of the eight level "clear word" phase of knowledge. [9]

Interestingly enough, the Africans of Kemet also assigned great significance to the Sirius System. Kemet, being the birthplace of our modern calendar, had a calendar that contained 365 and a quarter days based on their astronomical observation. A year is the time it takes for the earth to revolve around the sun. Currently, we adjust for the quarter of a day by having a leap year every four years, in which a day is added to the calendar. In other words, the quarter of a day that is not accounted for on our calendars each year is reconciled every four years with the addition of a day. (1/4 day a year times four years equal 1 day.)

In yet another instance of brilliance, the people of Kemet knew that every 1, 460 years the heliacal rising of Sirius would take place. Therefore, instead of adjusting their calendar every four years by one day, they would adjust for a year every 1,460 years! With a quarter of a day discrepancy per year, by the time 1,460 years has passed, the quarter days will have added up to 365 days! (1,460 times 1/4 day per year = 365 days.) The heliacal rising of Sirius was then the day upon which the adjustment was to be made to reconcile the civic calendar(365 days) with the astronomical calendar (365 1/4 days). As can be imagined, a tremendous amount of astronomical sophistication and meticulous coordination was necessary to manage and observe a cyclical time span of 1,460 years. Diop noted that this calendar was in use as early as 4,236 years B.C. Given this date and the fact that many cycles would have to be observed to establish a pattern, they could have been making their astronomical observations as early as 8,616 years B.C., a time period that allows for only three cyclic observations of Sirius over 1460 years per cycle. This is something that Americans cannot fathom because compared to Kemet, America is a fetus society of a little over 200 years of age. However, the people of Kemet were an old enough society and a sophisticated enough society to manage this time period.

> the Pharaoh had created a national service presided over by
> the great vizier, the highest official of the Egyptian state, and devoted
> exclusively to the observation of the rising of Sirius: thus the Egyptian
> astronomers had made tables that allowed, each year, the monitoring of
> the gap between the year of the civil and of the astronomical calendars
> on which historic events were projected... [10]

The connections between the ancients in Kemet and the more contemporary Dogons, regarding Sirius, are more than coincidence. First, the holistic interpretation and use of knowledge is a part of the cultural unity of Africa. Consequently, it is commonplace to find stellar symbolism and observation in Africa's many diverse societies. Secondly, it is likely that there was some contact and sharing of information between the ancient Dogon and ancient Kemet. In fact, given the vast migrations of Africans across the continent at different periods in time, as well as linguistic and other similarities such as those Diop recognized between Wolof and the language of Kemet, there is the possibility that among the Dogon are some of the descendants of ancient Kemet.

Whatever the case, we find that Africa, far from being the dark continent that many people have been misinformed to believe, is in fact full of enlightenment. Africa is more than able to present models for our present and future nation building.

Even before Kemet, the framework for that civilization had been laid in Nubia/Kush/Ethiopia. Evidence continues to mount concerning the place of Nubia as the mother of Kemet. Not only has archeological evidence shown articles in Nubia that predate those in Kemet, but these articles show parallels to what was to appear later in Kemet. For example, figurines with the royal flail, crook and garments particular to Kemet were found in Nubian sites that predate the dynastic period of Kemet, which arguable began around 3100 B.C.. The people of Kemet also admittedly "looked to the south" for their origins.

Nubia also thrived as a contemporary of Kemet. During many times in the history of Kemet, Nubian pharaohs held the throne. Queen Amhose Nefertari and Queen Tiye were two of such rulers from Nubia during the 18th Dynasty. Of course, their progeny necessarily are also Nubian. Queen Amhose Nefertari was the mother of a daughter also named Amhose. This daughter, Amhose, was a wife of Thutmosis I. Amhose and Thutmosis I had a daughter who is one of the most well known rulers of Kemet. That daughter was Queen Hatshepsut, the builder of the great funerary bearing her name. Queen Tiye, one of the most beautiful African figures one can see in Kemet, was the mother of King Akhenaton (Amenhotep IV). Even the king that the West has made famous, Tutankhamun, is believed to have either been the son of Queen Tiye or the son of Akhenaton. Given the structure of royal families, with multiple wives and many children, it is easy to see how Nubian rulers were inextricably interwoven into Kemet, especially in times like the 18th Dynasty.

Later in the history of Kemet during a time of societal trouble and foreign rule, the parent of Kemet came to the rescue in the form of the Nubian ruler Kashta. The Nubians drove the foreigners out of Kemet and assumed the leadership positions. Two sons of Kashta were Shabaka and

Piankhy. Piankhy was a leader of tremendous military genius and reverence for the traditions and religion of Kemet. His son Taharka also ruled in Kemet from the throne in Napata, Nubia. It is clear that we must add the ancients of Nubia/Kush/Ethiopia to the model we are building. In fact, in the Southern parts of modern day Kemet, such as Aswan, Nubians still live and speak the Nubian language.

In addition to the Dogon, many West African civilizations have much to offer our model. The most well known of these are Ghana, Mali, and Songhay. The apexes of these three empires ran from around 700 A.D. to 1600 A.D. During this time, which encompassed the time of the European Dark Ages,

> In the principal cities of West Africa, such as Gao, Jenne, and Timbuktu, universities and other educational institutions were established, and their level of scholarship was of a high caliber. In the schools, colleges, and universities of the Songhay Empire, courses were given in astronomy, mathematics, ethnography, medicine, hygiene, philosophy, logic, prosody, diction, elocution, rhetoric, and music. Professor Ahmed Baba, of the faculty of the University of Sankore, in Timbuktu, was a scholar of vast erudition. [11]

John Jackson also speaks specifically about Jenne, when he writes that "Their medical school trained physicians and surgeons of great skill. Among the difficult surgical operations performed successfully by doctors in Jenne was the removal of cataracts from the human eye." [12] Chancellor Williams tells us of the similar intellectual heights reached in Timbuktu at the University of Sankore.

> The University structure consisted of a (1) Faculty of Law, (2) Medicine and surgery, (3) Letters, (4) Grammar, (5) Geography, and (6) Art (Here "Art" had to do with such practical training as manufacturing, building and other allied crafts. After the basic training the expertise required was through the traditional apprenticeship system in the various craft guilds). There were thousands of students from all parts of West Africa and other regions. We have no record of the exact number. The accounts also mention the large number of scientists, doctors, lawyers and other scholars... [13]

Also in roughly the same time period as Ghana, Mali, and Songhay, from 700 A.D. to 1200 A.D., Makuria was yet another thriving African culture situated to the South of Kemet. The splendor of Makuria was described by visitors as:

> ... magnificent stone and brick palaces, temples, churches, cathedrals, wide avenues lined with palm trees, government buildings, public baths, water supply systems, beautiful gardens, countless craft industries, huge farms with extensive pastures where camels, horses, oxen, cows, sheep, goats and pigs could be seen grazing lazily... [14]

This is our model. This amalgamation of genius in our own African image is what we need to emulate and study as a point of departure for our standards and paradigms. We need look no further than ourselves for the answers we seek. From Nubia to Makuria, and many unmentioned examples in between, Africa is rich with greatness. The sons and daughters of the Maafa must realize that this greatness is locked within each of us. We must only unlock it by first gaining the knowledge of this greatness and then acting accordingly. That is what the term "knowledge is power" is supposed to mean. When we know ourselves and our history, and we are moved to build and create based on our heightened consciousness and African historical models, knowledge truly becomes power.

As we come out of the Maafa and its aftermath we move forward seeking knew models of how to build our African nation. Whether we raise the flag and wave the colors of the red, black and green as a conceptually and ancestrally united people or in a new African nation with territory and national borders, we need models and paradigms to follow. To date in the history of the world there is none better than the ancient African model.

CONCLUSION

There comes a time in the existence of a people when they must come face to face with the truth. They must deal head on with themselves, their immediate existence, their past and their future. There can be little room for romanticism, lies and sleeping minds. The Maafa was real and its aftermath is real as painful as it may be to confront. Individuals will be forced through the cycle of world events to wake up and rise, or go down, acting as complacent or conscious partners with the destructive forces of this world.

The lies, distortions, omissions and downright criminal behavior of today's supremacist societies are going down. When I say supremacist societies I mean any societies built upon the Maafa or any other misuse, misducation and murder of masses of people. Most, if not all of today's so called Westerm powers fit the profile of supremacist and all of them are unwilling to change their ways sufficiently to reverse their fate. Do not fool yourself into thinking that this does not include America. It is a fact that America is built upon the foundations that fit the definition of supremacist, White supremacist to be specific, and will crumble "For being out of harmony with the order of heaven, earth and society, i.e., Maat, is to invite destruction." [1] The task now is to crucially assess ourselves and what we as individuals and a collective must do to rise above the destructive ways of the world.

African people are at a crossroads. These are the times indicative of the calm before the storm. We must build our ark. We must study our history and learn from the Maafa so that we can better interpret the present turmoil we are in, refusing to be the sufferer any longer. Create and build so that the coming storm, the now cyclic European assault on African people and our own self-destruction, will be as weak as a feather is light against our foundations. Unify, so that we are sheltered together from the gathering storm. Why get off the ground after being knocked down, if you can avoid the blow altogether and counter in defense of your life?

Just as Europe went through her Dark Ages, we, African people, are in our Dark Age now. The masses of our people are suffering. Brothers and sisters languish in what we call ghettos and projects, but are actually colonies. Just as Europe has colonized Africa in the wake of the Maafa, creating dependent people controlled from outside of their community, America has the huddled masses existing in colonies called the inner city; with more police brutality than South Africa, crime against one another and suffering a modern day enslavement.

One of the major differences between our Dark Age and that of Europe is that Europeans were responsible for falling into their own and came out of it with the assistance of knowledge wielding Africans and Arabs. Today Europeans, largely through the Maafa, are responsibe for our Dark Age and we must bring ourselves out of it.

This book is yet another of the many calls to consciousness needed to begin our ascent. Hopefully it has offered an overall historical picture, making unity logical and necessary. Sterling Stuckey gives us something to think further on in a passage from his book *Slave Culture*.

> During the process of their becoming a people, Yorubas, Akans, Ibos, Angolans, and others were present on slave ships to America and experienced a common horror--unearthly moans and piercing shrieks, the smell of filth and the stench of death, all during the violent rythms and quiet coursings of ships at sea. As such, slave ships were the first real incubators of slave unity across cultural lines, cruelly revealing irreducible links from one ethnic group to the other, fostering resistance thousands of miles before the shores of the new land appeared on the horizon--before there was mention of natural rights in North America. [2]

As we ponder the initial unity that African people forged as a result of a common experience of oppression, it should be so that we move again to that level of unity in the context of today. We as an African people around the world share the common burden of oppression which must be our catalyst for the unification of our present day masses. If this book has not at least begun the process of stirring brain activity towards further contemplation and a realization of our unity, for even the least conscious of our brothers in sisters, it has failed in that regard. However, this work has also reclaimed our history and exercised the freedom of maximally using language to the benefit of our mental and physical liberation. The word Maafa frames our experience in the language and context that heals, protects and enpowers African people, simply by its utterance. In this respect, if you have picked up this book and only read and understood the title, it can be called a success.

It is further hoped that with the perspective of the Maafa offered here, a new paradigm has been set for the way we deal with our suffering and hold perpetrators of oppression accountable. Whenever we refer to our enslavement it should be called the Maafa or Great Suffering. Whether in casual conversations, classrooms, presentations of writings, we need to frame our experience in our terms using the words Maafa or Great Suffering. This is about the mental attitudes and actions that we possess as a people to rise once again to the level of peace, prosperity, harmony and balance that the greatness of our ancestors and our history dictates.

We have our work laid before us. It is now our test to see whether we will act or go down in history as the most foolish people to walk the earth; people who had an opportunity to return to their former greatness and did not do it. I truly hope that our decision is to rise.

The hopeful aspect of our struggle is that even if many decide not to rise, their will still be those of us who rise in an attempt to uplift ourselves and our people. There is much hope. Looking at the fact that as many of us survived the Maafa as did, this is a testament in itself to our strength. Then, if we look at how so many have been the brightest minds and most vital champions for humanity, in spite of the Maafa, we have shown that we can rise.

We have much to be proud of as a people. We have been through the fire and even though we are not yet out of it, we can still draw inspiration from how far we have come. We MUST recapture the knowledge and spirit that made us great once before. Our unity is a must. Our continued enlightenment is a must. Our African cultural aesthetic is a must. Raising the flag and waving the colors is a must.

Finally, let us close with a reminder of our suffering.

> Slaves were sometimes whipped till they were blistered and bloodied and then the blisters would be "cut open on a slaves back, dripped sealing wax into them, poured a solution of fiery peppers onto the sores, or aggrevated the lacerations by striking them with a hand saw. [3]

This is the Maafa. WE MUST NEVER FORGET, but move on African people... move on.

Notes

Introduction

1. The term, African people, is used to refer to Africans on the continent, as well as African descendants in North America, South America, the Carribean and wherever else they may exist. There is no distinction between African and African American, African Brazilian, etc.

2. Maulana Karenga and Jacob Carruthers, eds., <u>Kemet and the African Worldview: Research, Rescue and Restoration</u> (Los Angeles: University of Sankore Press, 1986), p. 106.

3. Maulana Karenga, <u>Selections from the Husia: Sacred Wisdom of Ancient Egypt</u> (Los Angeles: University of Sankore Press, 1984), p. 5.

4. Marimba Ani, <u>Yurugu: An African-Centered Critique of European Cultural Thought and Behavior</u> (Trenton: Africa World Press, Inc., 1994), p. xxi.

5. Haki Madhubuti, <u>Claiming Earth: Race, Rage, Rape, Redemption; Blacks Seeking a Culture of Enlightened Empowerment</u> (Chicago: Third World Press, 1994), p. 37.

6. Na'im Akbar, <u>Chains and Images of Psychological Slavery</u> (Jersey City: New Mind Productions, 1984), p. 7.

Chapter 1

1. John Henrik Clarke, <u>Christopher Columbus & the Afrikan Holocaust: Slavery and the Rise of European Capitalism</u> (New York: A & B Books Publishers, 1992), p. 100.

2. Joseph Inikori, The Chaining of a Continent: Export Demand for Captives and the History of Africa South of the Sahara, 1450-1870 (Kingston, Jamaica: Institute for Social and Economic Research, 1992), p. 5.

3. David Henige, "A Skeptical View of How Much Can Be Known," in The Atlantic Slave Trade, ed. David Northrup (Lexington, Massachusetts: D.C. Heath and Company, 1994), p. 60.

4. Philip D. Curtin, The African Slave Trade (Madison, Wisconsin: University of Wisconsin Press, 1969), p. xviii.

5. Inikori, pp. 4-5.

6. Curtin, pp. 15-16.

7. James A. Rawley, The Trans-Atlantic Slave Trade (New York: Norton, 1981), p. 324.

8. Paul E. Lovejoy, "Curtin's Calculations Refined But Not Refuted," in The Atlantic Slave Trade, ed. David Northrup (Lexington, Massachusetts: D.C. Heath and Company, 1994), p. 54.

9. Joseph Inikori, "A Skpetical View of Curtin's and Lovejoy's Calculations," in The Atlantic Slave Trade, ed. David Northrup (Lexington, Massachusetts: D.C. Heath and Company, 1994), p. 66.

10. Rawley, p. 428.

11. Curtin, Table 77.

12. Lerone Bennett, Jr., Before the Mayflower: A History of Black America, Sixth Edition (New York: Penguin Books, 1993), p. 29.

13. Joseph C. Miller, "Deaths Before the Middle Passage," in The Atlantic Slave Trade, ed. David Northrup (Lexington, Massachusetts: D.C. Heath and Company, 1994), pp. 123-124.

14. Basil Davidson, Black Mother; Africa: the years of trial (The African Slave Trade) (London: V. Gollancz, 1968), p. 88.

15. Ibid, p. 88.

Chapter 2

1. Julius Lester, To Be A Slave (New York: Dial Books for Young Readers, 1968), p. 33.

2. Six Women's Slave Narratives (New York: Oxford University Press, 1988), p.7.

3. Olaudah Equino, "Kidnapped, Enslaved, and Sold Away, c. 1756," in The Atlantic Slave Trade, ed. David Northrup (Lexington, Massachusetts: D.C. Heath and Company, 1944), pp. 78-79.

4. Lester, p. 43.

5. Lester, p. 38.

6. Six Women's Slave Narratives, p. 11.

7. Ibid, p. 12.

8. John Newton, "Reformed Slave Trader's Regrets, c. 1745-1754," in The Atlantic Slave Trade, ed. David Northrup (Lexington, Massachusetts: D.C. Heath Company, 1994), p. 87.

9. Ibid, p. 85.

10. John W. Blassingame, The Slave Community: Plantation Life in the Antebellum South, Revised & Enlarged Edition (New York: Oxford University Press, 1979), p. 172.

11. Ibid, p. 154.

12. Ibid.

13. Lerone Bennett, Jr., Before the Mayflower: A History of Black America, Sixth Edition (New York: Penguin Books, 1993), p. 53.

Chapter 3

1. George Frasier, Success Runs in Our Race: The Complete Guide to Effective Networking in the African-American Community (New York: Morrow & Company, 1994), pp. 65-67.

2. John Henrik Clarke, preface to Africans in Brazil: A Pan-African Perspective, by Abdias Do Nascimento and Elisa Larkin Nascimento (Trenton: Africa World Press, Inc., 1992), p. v.

3. Colin Palmer, "Afro-Mexican Culture and Consciousness During the Sixteenth and Seventeeth Centuries," in Global Dimensions of the African Diaspora, Second Edition, ed. Joseph E. Harris (Washington, D.C: Howard University Press, 1993), p. 126.

4. Charles Joyner, Down By The Riverside: A South Carolina Slave Community (Urbana: University of Illinois Press, 1984), p. 198.

5. Ibid, p. 207.

6. William Bascom, "Gullah Folk Beliefs Concerning Child Birth," in Sea Island Roots: African Presence in the Carolinas & Georgia, ed. Kenneth E. Baird and Mary A. Twining (Trenton: Africa World Press, Inc., 1991), p. 27.

7. Kenneth E. Baird and Mary A. Twining, "Names and naming in the Sea Islands," in Sea Island Roots: African Presence in the Carolinas & Georgia, ed. Kenneth E. Baird and Mary A. Twining (Trenton: Africa World Press, Inc., 1991), p. 40.

8. Janie Gilliard Moore, "A James Island Childhood: Africanisms Among Families of the Sea Islands of Charleston, South Carolina," in Sea Island Roots: African Presence in the Carolinas & Georgia, ed. Kenneth E. Baird and Mary A. Twining (Trenton: Africa World Press, Inc., 1991), p. 108.

9. Abdias Do Nascimento and Elisa Larkin Nascimento, Africans in Brazil: A Pan-African Perspective (Trenton: Africa World Press, Inc., 1992), p. 63.

10. Migene Gonzalez-Wippler, Santeria: The Religion (New York: Harmony Books, 1989).

11. Yosef A. A. ben-Jochannan, <u>African Origins of the Major Western Religions</u> (Baltimore: Black Classic Press, 1991), p. 65.

12. George Brandon, "Sacrificial Practices in Santeria, an African-Cuban Religion in the United States," in <u>Africanisms in American Culture</u>, First Midland Book Edition, ed. Joseph E. Holloway (Bloomington: Indiana University Press, 1991), p. 123.

13. Jesse Gaston Mulira, "The Case of Voodoo in New Orleans," in <u>Africanisms in American Culture</u>, First Midland Book Edition, ed. Joseph E. Calloway (Bloomington: Indiana University Press, 1991), pp. 34-35.

14. Leonard E. Barrett, Sr., <u>The Rastafarians</u> (Boston: Beacon Press Books, 1988), p. 121.

15. Ibid, p. 16.

16. Ibid, p. 17.

17. Joyce Elaine King and Thomasyne Lightfoote Wilson, "BEing the Soul-Freeing Substance: A Legacy of Hope in AfroHumanity," in <u>Too Much Schooling, Too Little Education: A Paradox of Black Life in White Societies</u>, ed. Mwalimu Shujaa (Trenton: Africa World Press, Inc., 1994), p. 276.

Chapter 4

1. Beverly J. Armento, et al, <u>America Will Be</u> (Boston: Houghton Mifflin, 1991), p. 412.

2. Houghton Mifflin Company, <u>The American Heritage Dictionary of the English Language</u>, 3rd Edition (Boston, 1992).

3. Lerone Bennett, Jr., <u>Before the Mayflower: A History of Black America</u>, Sixth Edition (New York: Penguin Books, 1993), p. 113.

4. Ibid, p. 126.

5. Columbus Salley, The Black 100: A Ranking of the Most Influential African-Americans, Past and Present (New York: Citadel Press, Carol Publishing Group, 1993), p. 12.

6. David Walker, Walker's Appeal, in Four Articles: Together With A Preamble, to the Coloured Citizens of the World, but in particular, and very expressly, to those of the United States of America (New York: Hill and Wang, 1965), pp. 25-26.

7. Salley, p. 58.

Chapter   5

1. Joseph Inikori, The Chaining of a Continent: Export Demand for Captives and the History of Africa South of the Sahara, 1450-1870 (Kingston, Jamaica: Institute for Social and Economic Research, 1992), p. 2.

2. David Northrup, ed. The Atlantic Slave Trade (Lexington, Massachusetts: D.C. Heath and Company, 1994), p. xiii.

3. J.D. Fage and Roland Oliver, eds. The Cambridge History of Africa, Vol. 6 1870-1905 (Cambridge: Cambridge University Press, 1985), p. 133.

4. Ibid, p. 261.

5. Chancellor Williams, The Rebirth of African Civilization (Chicago: Third World Press, 1993), p. 185.

6. Ibid, p. 186.

7. W.E. Burghardt DuBois, The World and Africa: An inquiry into the part which Africa has played in world history, New Enlarged Edition (New York: International Publishers, 1965), p. 266.

8. John Henrik Clarke, Notes for an African World Revolution: Africans at the Crosswords (Trenton: Africa World Press, Inc., 1991), p. 199.

Chapter 6

1. Chancellor Williams, The Rebirth of African Civilization (Chicago: Third World Press, 1993), pp. 210-211.

2. Chancellor Williams, The Destruction of Black Civilization: Great Issues of a Race from 4500 B.C. to 2000 A. D. (Chicago: Third World Press, 1987), p. 341.

3. Joyce Elaine King and Thomasyne Lightfoote Wilson, "BEing the Soul-Freeing Substance: A Legacy of Hope in AfroHumanity," in Too Much Schooling, Too Little Education: A Paradox of Black Life in White Societies, ed. Mwalimu Shujaa (Trenton: Africa World Press, Inc., 1994), p. 286.

4. Ivan Van Sertima, ed. Great African Thinkers: Cheikh Anta Diop (New Brunswick: Transaction Books, 1986), p. 8.

5. Ibid, p. 10.

6. Cheikh Anta Diop, Black Africa: The Economic and Cultural Basis for a Federated State, Africa World Press Edition (Trenton: Africa World Press, 1987), p. 88.

7. Ibid

8. John Henrik Clarke, Notes for an African World Revolution: Africans at the Crossroads (Trenton: Africa World Press, Inc., 1991), p. 398.

9. Houghton Mifflin Company, The American Heritage Dictionary of the English Language, 3rd Edition (Boston, 1992), p. 1826.

10. Holly Sklar, ed., Trilateralism: The Trilateral Commission and Elite Planning for World Management (Boston: South End Press, 1980), p. 41.

11. Ibid

12. Ibid, p. 39.

13. Haki Madhubuti, Black Men: Obsolete, Single, Dangerous? (Chicago: Third World Press, 1990), p. 218.

Chapter 7

1. James A. Banks, <u>An Introduction to Multicultural Education</u> (Needham Heights, Massachusetts: Allyn and Bacon, 1994).

2. Agyei Akoto, "Notes on an Afrikan-Centered Pedagogy," in <u>Too Much Schooling, Too Little Education: A Paradox of Black Life in White Societies</u>, ed. Mwalimu Shujaa (Trenton: Africa World Press, Inc., 1994), p. 322.

Chapter 8

1. Kwame Ture & Charles V. Hamilton, <u>Black Power: The Politics of Liberation</u>, Vintage Edition (New York: Random House, Vintage Books, 1992), p. 35.

2. Ibid

3. Houghton Mifflin Company, <u>The American Heritage Dictionary of the English Langauge</u>, 3rd Edition (Boston, 1992), p. 1909.

4. Ibid, p. 1203.

5. Ibid, p. 1865.

Chapter 9

1. Timothy Wheeler, "Third World Horrors: Sign of Scarcity?: Experts Split on Role of Population Growth," <u>Baltimore Sun</u>, 14 August 1994, 1E.

2. Ibid, 4E.

3. Ibid

4. Margaret Udansky, "Birth control, abortion are tough issues," <u>U.S.A. Today</u>, 31 August 1994, 2A.

5. Tom Squitieri, "Africa's Quandry: More People, less food," U.S.A. Today, 31 August 1994, 2A.

Chapter 10

1. Arrested Development, "Africa's inside me," Zingalamaduni, Chrysalis Records, 1994. Audiocassette.

2. Ibid.

3. Arrested Development, "Ease my mind," Zingalamaduni, Chrysalis Records, 1994. Audiocassette.

4. Tonya Pendleton and Frank Dexter Brown, "Conscious Minds," YSB, Oct. 1994, 32.

5. Boogie Down Productions, Edutainment, Zomba Recording Corp., 1990. Audiocassette.

6. Boogie Down Productions, "Why is That?," Zomba Recording Corp., 1989. Cassette Single.

7. Boogie Down Productions, "Exhibit A," Eductainment, Zomba Recording Corp., 1990. Audiocassette.

8. Boogie Down Productions, "Blackman in Effect," Edutainment, Zomba Recording Corp., 1990. Audiocassette.

9. X-Clan, "Funkin' Lesson," To the East Blackwards, Island Records, Inc., 1990. Audiocassette.

10. Ibid.

11. X-Clan, "Grand Verbalizer, What Time Is It?," To the East Blackwards, Island Records, Inc., 190. Audiocassette.

12. X-Clan, "Tribal Jam," To the east Blackwards, Island Records, Inc., 1990. Audiocassette.

13. Public Enemy, "Fight the Power," Fear of a Black Planet, CBS

Records, Inc., 1990. Audiocassette.

14. Public Enemy, <u>Muse Sick-N-Hour Mess Age</u>, Def Jam Recordings, 1994. Audiocassette.

15. Sule Greg Wilson, <u>The Drummers Path: Moving the Spirit with Ritual and Traditional Drumming</u> (Rochester, Vermont: Destint Books, 1992), p. 21.

Chapter 11

1. Na'im Akbar, <u>Chains and Images of Psychological Slavery</u> (Jersey City, New Jersey: New Mind Productions, 1984), p. 2.

2. Robert Berkow, M.D., editor-in-chief, <u>The Merck Manual of Diagnosis and Therapy</u> (Rahway, New jersey: Merck Research Laboratories, 1992), p. 1833.

3. Ibid, p. 1835.

4. Ibid, p. 1587.

5. Ibid.

6. Ibid, p. 1589.

7. Houghton Mifflin Company, <u>The American Heritage Dictionary of the English Language</u>, 3rd Edition (Boston, 1992), p. 303.

8. Ibid, p. 6.

9. Lerone Bennett, Jr., <u>The Shaping of Black America: The Struggles and Triumphs of African Americans, 1619 to the 1990's</u> (New York: Penguin Books, 1993), p. 148.

10. Carter G. Woodson, <u>The Mis-Education of the Negro</u> Africa World Press, Inc. edition (Trenton, New Jersey: Africa World Press, Inc., 1990), p. 17.

11. George M. Frederickson, <u>The Black Image in the White Mind: The Debate on Afro-American Character and Destiny, 1817-1914</u> (New York: Harper & Row Publishers, 1971), p. xii.

12. Berkow, p. 1545.

13. Aurthur M. Schlesinger, Jr., <u>The Disuniting of America: Reflections on a Multicultural Society</u> (New York: W.W. Norton & Company, 1992), p. 127.

14. Frederickson, p. 232.

15. Berkow, p. 1546.

16. David Van Biema, "When White Makes Right: Skinheads carve out their niche in America's violent culture of hate," <u>Time</u>, 9 Aug. 1993, p. 41.

17. Berkow, pp. 1547-1548.

18. Francis Cress Welsing, M.D., <u>The Isis Papers: The Keys to the Colors</u> (Chicago: Third World Press, 1991), p. ii.

19. Marimba Ani, <u>Yurugu: An African-Centered Critique of European Cultural Thought and Behavior</u> (Africa World Press, Inc., 1994), pp. 39-40.

20. Ibid, p. 492.

Chapter 12

1. Shelby Steele, <u>The Content of Our Character: A New Vision of Race in America</u>, First Harper Perennial edition (New York: HarperPerennial, 1991), p. 173.

2. Houghton Mifflin Company, <u>The American Heritage Dictionary of the English Language</u>, 3rd Edition (Boston, 1992), p. 112.

3. Maulana Karenga, <u>Introduction to Black Studies</u> (Los Angeles: University of Sankore Press, 1982), p. 292.

Chapter 14

1. Houghton Mifflin Company, <u>The American Heritage Dictionary of the English Language</u>, 3rd Edition (Boston, 1992), p. 349.

2. Chancellor Williams, <u>The Rebirth of African Civilization</u> (Chicago: Third World Press, 1993), p. 89.

3. Cheikh Anta Diop, <u>Black Africa: The Economic and Cultural Basis for a Federated State</u>, Africa World Press Edition (Trenton: Africa World Press, Inc., 1987), p. 24.

4. Asa Hilliard, "Pedagogy in Ancient Kemet," in <u>Kemet and the African Worldview: Research, Rescue and Restoration</u>, eds. Maulana Karenga and Jacob H. Carruthers (Los Angeles: University of Sankore Press, 1986), p. 137.

5. George G. M. James, <u>Stolen Legacy: Greek Philosophy is Stolen Egyptian Philosophy</u> (1954; reprint, Newport News, Va: United Brothers Communications Systems, 1989), p. 135.

6. Hilliard, p. 139.

7. James, p. 135.

8. Anthony Browder, <u>Nile Valley Contribution to Civilization</u>, Exploding the Myths Vol. 1 (Washington, D.C: Institute of Karmic Guidance, 1992), p. 106.

9. Hunter Adams III, "African Observers of the Universe: The Sirius Question," in <u>Blacks in Science: Ancient and Modern</u>, ed. Ivan Van Sertima (New Brunswick: Transaction Books, 1983), p. 28.

10. Cheikh Anta Diop, <u>Civilization or Barbarism: An Authentic Anthropolgy (Civilisation ou Barbarie)</u>, trans. Yaa-Lengi Meema Ngemi (New York: Lawrence Hill Books, 1991), p. 280.

11. John G. Jackson, <u>Introduction to African Civilizations</u>, 1st Carol Publisher Group Edition (New York: Carol Publishing Group, Citadel Press, 1990), p. 217.

12. Ibid, p. 215.

13. Chancellor Williams, <u>The Destruction of Black Civilization: Great Issues of a Race from 4500 B.C. to 2000 A. D.</u> (Chicago: Third World Press, 1987), p. 205.

14. Ibid, p. 149.

Conclusion

1. Ivan Van Sertima, ed., <u>Egypt Revisited</u> (New Brunswick, New Jersey: Transaction Publishers, 1989), p. 373.

2. Sterling Stuckey, <u>Slave Culture: Nationalist Theory and the Foundations of Black America</u> (New York: Oxford University Press, 1987), p. 3.

3. Paul D. Essot, <u>Slavery Remembered: A Record of 20th Century Slave Narratives</u> (Chapel Hill, North Carolina: University of North Carolina Press, 1979)